SUPREME COURT.

RICE A. BEAL,
Appellee.

vs.

ALVAN W. CHASE AND THE ANN ARBOR PRINTING AND PUBLISHING COMPANY,
Appellants.

Appeal from Washtenaw Circuit Court. In Chancery.

Argument of H. J. Beakes, for Defendants.

LAWRENCE & SAWYER,
Solicitors for Appellants.
GEORGE V. N. LOTHROP AND HIRAM J. BEAKES,
Of Counsel, for Appellants.

Supreme Court -- At Lansing.

RICE A. BEAL,
   Complainant,
    vs.
ALVAN W. CHASE, and THE ANN ARBOR PRINTING and PUBLISHING COMPANY,
      Defendants.

STATEMENT OF THE CASE.

About August 30th, 1869, the defendant, Chase, sold and conveyed to the complainant real estate in Ann Arbor, on which there was a dwelling-house and a brick building called " Dr. Chase's Steam Printing House." At the same time Dr. Chase sold to Beal the following property as described in the contract, viz: " The machinery, boiler, engine, presses, tools, furniture and stock of whatever name or nature, in the building occupied by said Chase as his steam printing office and this day sold by him," to said Beal, " together with all the accounts for unfinished work on which payment has not already been made, together with the subscription list of the Peninsular Courier and Family Visitant, and also the copyright to a book called ' Dr. Chase's Recipes, or Information for Everybody;" and also another book called ' The Judd Family ;' also a book called ' Reminescences of a Voyage around the World,' a copyright of which is hereafter to be obtained, together with the good will of the business of printing and publishing, and also the right to use the name of Dr. Chase in connection with said books, and all the stereotype and electro plates for said books now completed, and also all the book-bindery tools and stock and all contracts for printing and publishing, together with all moneys hereafter to be received upon jobs or work unfinished."

The contract between Chase and Beal was in writing and under seal and contained the following covenant: "And the said party of the first part, (Dr. Chase,) also agrees that while said Beal remains in said business of printing and publishing in Ann Arbor, he will not, either directly or indirectly, engage in the business of printing and publishing in the State of Michigan."

The contract further provided that "said Beal is to have the privilege of receiving the letters connected with said business, and opening the same." See Contract, pp. 53, 77, 452.

The bill sets out this contract in substance, together with what it alleges to have been the negotiations between Chase and Beal relating to the purchase, together with alleged parol assurances and promises on the part of Chase, which are introduced into the bill for the apparent purpose of enlarging the contract. I say *parol* promises, because I think that is the fair though not very distinct import of the bill, and because the evidence clearly shows that the whole *written* contract between the parties is the one of which "Exhibit B," annexed to the answers of the defendants, on pages 53 and 57 of Record, and which was put in evidence by complainant as "Exhibit No. 2," (see page 452,) the substance of which I have quoted above.

The parol promises alleged in the bill are that "it was understood and agreed between them, (meaning between Chase and Beal) that to enable your orator to enjoy the full benefit of his purchase of the copyright of said book," (meaning "Dr. Chase's Recipes, or Information for Everybody,") and of the good will which said Chase had secured in the sale of the same, and the arrangements made by him for such sales, that all letters which should come addressed to him, said Chase, at said post-office and not inscribed with the number of his private box should be delivered to your orator at said office and be opened by him, and that he should retain all said letters as related to said book or any matters pertaining to the business aforesaid, to enable your orator to receive and appropriate to his own use all such remittances, whether the same were money, drafts or post-office orders, and to write said Chase's name whenever necessary in connection therewith, your orator to deliver or send to said Chase such of the letters received as should be found on inspection to have no relation to said book or business:" (See page 5:) and on page 7, after alleging certain "*representations*" during the negotiations, the bill proceeds to state: "and he further assured your orator and agreed with him that upon said sale being made, *he would not only retire altogether from such business*, but would aid your orator in said business, and especially in the sale of said book, by his advice and counsel, and all the means in his power, and that he would devote the next six months, at least, with his personal services for that purpose, and would continue thereafter to do what he could to promote your orator's interest in such business, and to make the sale and publication of said pook profitable to your orator."

The answer of Dr. Chase admits the making of the written contract and sets out a full copy of it, (being "Exhibit B," page 53,) and a copy of the deed, ("Exhibit A," page 51, and avers that such written contract and deed constituted the entire contract, pages 31 and 35. He avers that at the time of the sale he had no private post-office box, (aside from the Peninsular Courier drawer, in which the exchanges of the newspaper and Chase's mail had been received previous to the sale,) and that after the sale was consummated, on some day subsequent to the delivery of the deed and contract, he " as a mere matter of courtesy and convenience to the complainant, and without any consideration to Chase or obligation on his part to do so, and in contemplation of a temporary absence of said Chase from Ann Arbor, verbally consented that Beal might receive and open all letters which should come addressed to Chase at the post-office, but that he had no thought or intention of surrendering permanently, to complainant or any other person, the right of opening his correspondence generally, and never received any consideration for any such surrender, but that the concent he gave was a mere temporary license and subject to revocation at any time, except so far as letters addressed to him are governed by said written contract of which " Exhibit B." is a copy. See pages 35, 36 and 37.

He denies making any agreement to retire altogether from the business or to aid the complainant as alleged in the bill, or to devote the next six months of his personal service, or that he would continue thereafter to do what he could to promote the complainant's interest in such business and to make said books profitable to complainant, but admits that he told complainant that if the purchase should be made, he, as a gratuity, would aid and assist Beal in his business for three months; and he avers that not a word was said by either party about Chase's retiring or restraining himself from engaging in the printing and publishing business until the purchase had been agreed on, the deeds and mortgages executed and assigned and the written contract was about half completed, when the complainant for the first time proposed that Chase should be restrained by contract from engaging in the printing and publishing business; and that he received no additional consideration for the restraint in the contract. He avers that the consideration price as finally received had been agreed upon and settled between him and Beal two days before the subject of restraining him from engaging in business was mentioned. Pages 41—42.

He denies that Beal was induced to believe by the representations stated in the bill, that in making the purchase, he, (Beal,) did or could acquire the exclusive right to the reputation of Chase, as author of said book, or that Chase would enter into no competition with him, &c. Page 60.

He insists that all the parol negotiations touching the contract which was reduced to writing were merged in the writing, or abandoned thereby. Page 32.

The bill alleges Chase's representations as to the extent of the business, and avers that such representations were true. Pages 3 and 4.

The material representations alleged in the bill as to the extent of the business of job printing, &c , are denied. See pages 32, 33, 34. He admits that the sales of the book, "Dr. Chase's Recipes, or Information for Everybody," previous to the close of 1868, had been over 325,000 copies. Page 33. He avers that the so-called "agents" for the sale of the book, were, in fact, direct purchasers from him for cash. Page 33.

The bill alleges that the consideration for the sale was sixty-five thousand dollars. The answer of Chase shows that the actual consideration was thirty-five thousand dollars in cash and securities treated as cash, and the remainder of the consideration was Minnesota real estate, called in the trade thirty thousand dollars, but of which the real value was only about six thousand dollars. Page 32.

The Ann Arbor Printing and Publishing Company is a corporation organized under the laws of the State of Michigan, August 26th, 1872, by articles of association executed on that day, and filed in the office of the Secreiary of State, August 28th, 1872, and in the office of the Clerk of Washtenaw county, August 30th, 1872. Record, p. 56 to 59, and 84 to 86.

The defendant Chase was one of the corporators, and until August 1st, 1873, was President, Superintendent, and a member of the Board of Directors. The other corporators were James C. Watson, Henry S. Dean, Sedgwick Dean, Henry Krause, and Zina P. King. All the corporators were members of the Board of Directors, and each had an equal voice in the Board. Until August 1st, 1873, James C. Watson was Vice-President, Zina P. King, Secretary, and Henry S. Dean the Treasurer of the company. Since that date James C. Watson has been the President, Henry Krause, Vice-President, H. S. Dean, Treasurer, and Zina P. King, Secretary. Dr. Chase, on the 1st day of August, 1873, sold to the other corporators his interest in the company, and retired from it in every capacity, and since that time, until November 18th, 1873, the only relation between Chase and the corporation was the royalty contract, of which "Exhibit C," page 54, is a copy. September 30th, 1873, the Ann Arbor Printing and Publishing Company assigned this royalty contract, of which "Exhibit C.," page 54, is a copy. September 30th, 1873, the Ann Arbor Printing and Publishing Company assigned this royalty contract to the Chase Publishing Company, of Toledo, Ohio, and on the 18th of November, 1873, Chase assented to the assignment. See Exhibit "A. A. 1," pp. 292, 480, 481. Since the last mentioned date no contract relations whatever have existed between Chase and the defendant corporation. Pp. 265, 266.

The bill alleges that about Dec. 1st, 1872, Chase, in violation of his agreement, engaged in the printing and publishing business in Ann Arbor, and is still so engaged, and has the charge and management of a large printing establishment, and has published and is still publishing books and a weekly newspaper, &c.; that such business is ostensibly carried on in the name and under the style of the Ann Arbor Printing and Publishing Company, which claims to be a corporation, organized under the laws of Michigan; but the complainant charges that Chase, after having threatened complainant that he would again engage in said business, promoted and caused the said corporation to be organized with the intention of evading his liability by the use of the corporate name; that the said organization consisted originally, and he believes still consists, of six stockholders; that Chase subscribed and owns one-half or more of the stock of the company; that Chase is the only one of the stockholders experienced in the business; that the six stockholders were and are the six directors of the corporation, but that it was the intention from the first that the company business should be under the care, supervision and direction of Chase: that before and at the time of the organization of the corporation, all the stockholders knew of Beal's purchase from Chase, and that Beal was still continuing the business under the name of "Dr. Chase's Steam Printing House," in Ann Arbor, and knew that Chase had entered into a contract with Beal in reference to the same, and had no right to establish and carry on such business at said city, directly or indirectly; and that Chase has had from the first the sole management of the business affairs of the company's establishment and has been and is its President and Superintendent.

The bill charges that Chase " has recently, as author, prepared another book entitled:

1873.   The New Book.   1873.

Dr. Chase's Family Physician, Farrier, Bee-Keeper and Second Receipt Book, being an entirely new and complete treatise," &c., and has caused such new book to be printed and published under his direct superintendence, but in the name of the Ann Arbor Printing and Publishing Company, at the establishment of the company in Ann Arbor, and that extensive efforts are being made for the sale of the new book throughout the country; that said

Chase and said company have sent a prospectus of the new book to persons acting as agents of the first book, with proposals for them to act as agents for the sale of the new book, and with a view of superceding the former book, and that they are each endeavoring by the use of the reputation of Dr. Chase and his first book, and the pretence that the second book contains full information on the same subjects, and is a better and more complete book than the first, and by the use of similar, and in some instances the same agencies to supercede the sale of the first book, and claims that Beal has a right to the good reputation of Chase as author, and to the arrangements made by Chase for the sale of the first book, and to such aid as Chase can render him, and that the course of Chase and the Ann Arbor corporation is in derogation of his rights, and if continued, will greatly impair or entirely destroy the sale of the book, the copyright of which was so purchased by him from Chase, and which he avers constituted a very material part of the consideration which induced him to purchase. Pp. 7, 8, 9.

The answers of both defendants and the uncontradicted evidence show that the Ann Arbor Printing and Publishing Company was organized without any reference to Beal's contract with Chase, and with no intent to evade any such contract; that Chase having had legal advice that the restraining contract was void, determined to go into the business before the corporation was formed, and had informed Beal of that intention at least one and a half years before, and had purchased some material and commenced setting type for his new book; that after the formation of the corporation, Chase transferred his new book and printing material to it in September, 1872, and that the defendant corporation not only ostensibly, but in reality and good faith had ever since carried on the printing and publishing business without concealment or cover. The answers deny the allegation of the bill, (and the uncontrodicted evidence sustains the denials,) that all the stockholders knew any restraining contract with Chase when the company was organized, and show that those stockholders who did know of his contract believed it to be void. Pp. 285, 286.

It clearly appears that the corporation is a genuine one; that all the stock was assessed alike, and that all the stockholders paid pro rata; that several of them engaged actively in the business of the corporation, King being the editor of the newspaper, and secretary of the corporation, Col. Dean being the treasurer, Professor Watson having been a practical printer, was the vice-president, and he and Sedgwick Dean were a standing committee to examine the books and supervise accounts; that Chase originally took half of the stock, and never had more than that, the other half having been taken by the other stockholders. Pp. 56 to 58, 266, 267, 292, 293.

    Professor Watson's testimony, pp. 392, 394, 395.
    Col. Dean's testimony,   " 404, 405, 406.
    Sedgwick Dean's testimony, " 412, 413, 414.
    Zina P. King's testimony,   " 427, 428, 429.
    Henry Krause' testimony,   " 439, 440.

Soon after Beal's purchase from Chase he changed the name of the establishment and imprint from "Dr. Chase's Steam Printing House" to "Courier Steam Printing House, R. A. Beal, proprietor."

    Chase's answer, pp. 40, 41.
    Company's answer, p. 67; also pp. 396, 406, 414.

The Ann Arbor corporation printed and published Chase's Second Receipt Book, under the contract of which "Exhibit C." annexed to the answer is a copy. Chase has caused that book to be published only by entering into that contract, though the work was done under his direct supervision and care in behalf of the corporation, but it was done in the regular course of the business of the company, and under the direction of its board of directors.

    Chase's answer, p. 45, also Company's answer.

The bill alleges that until the establishment of the printing and publishing office of the defendants, or about that time, *the complainant received the letters which came to the Ann Arbor post-office, directed to Chase, and opened the same,* and carried on all correspondence in reference to said book and business of "Dr. Chase's Printing House" without objection or hindrance, but that about said last mentioned time, Chase ordered the post-master not to deliver any letters coming to his address to complainant; that no such letters have been since delivered to complainant, but all directed to Chase have generally, as well as those directed to his private box, have been taken by Chase and opened by him; that for a short time after the time mentioned, Chase caused such letters as related to said business to be put into complainant's letter box, but since the publishing of the new book, to wit: about May 1st, 1873, said Chase has received all such letters and retained the same; that complainant believes that many letters pertaining to his book and business, and not directed to Chase's private box have been received by Chase, and that some of them contained money, some drafts, some post-office orders, and some were letters seeking for agencies for the sale of the first book, and others from persons who had previously been agents for the sale thereof; that said Chase, purporting to act as superintent of said company, replied to such letters and sent to such correspondents a descriptive circular of his new book. Pages 9 and 10.

The answer of Chase to these allegations of the bill is found on pages 36, 37, 46, 47 of the Record: and the answer of the company on pages 71 and 72. Each defendant denies having done anything in derogation of Beal's rights.

The other facts stated in the pleadings, as far as they be material in this case, can be more conveniently considered in more immediate connection with the points hereafter submitted.

The bill was filed July 14th, 1873, with *an exparte* order endorsed thereon, granted by the Circuit Judge, allowing an injunction in accordance with the prayer of the bill, except that the Ann Arbor Register was not to be interfered with by the injunction until the expiration of the time required by law for the publication of the legal notices then being published in such newspaper, (see page 14,) in conformity with which order the injunction, of which a copy appears on page 29, was issued and served on the defendants. And the record in the case shows that notwithstanding repeated efforts to obtain a dissolution or modification of the injunction, the defendant corporation, (as well as Chase,) was from that time until the first day of June, 1874, absolutely prohibited by the court below, not only from printing and publishing the second Receipt Book, but also from carrying on or engaging, either directly or indirectly, in the business of printing and publishing at all in the State of Michigan, (except during the brief suspension of the injunction as to the company for eight days in July, 1873, and except the publication of the newspaper for the few weeks required to complete legal advertisements as above stated), and this too without any reference to whether Chase should or should not cease to be in any way connected with the corporation, and under the sworn answers of defendants that he had ceased his conncetion as officer, corporator or employee in any capacity, and with full knowledge of the decision of this court, in Hubbard vs. Miller; and until September 1st, 1873, Chase was prohibited by injunction "from taking or receiving from the post-office in the city of Ann Arbor, *any letter or letters received at said office addressed to said Alvan W. Chase which shall not have on them a designation of the number of said Chase's private letter box at said office, or in any manner interfering to prevent the delivery of the same to the said Rice A. Beal at said office, and from appropriating to his use any such letters or infarmation therein contained, or any money, drafts or post-office money orders transmitted in or with any such letter*, thereby giving to Beal the first reading and exclusive use of Chase's entire correspondence on every subject and from all persons, except such letters as happened to have the number of his private box on the superscription and depriving him forever of the right to his own property if transmitted in an envelope not containing the talesmanic number.

The defendants noticed the case for hearing for every term of the court after issue joined. Some attempt at delay is shown by the record on the part of the complainant, but no attempt at diligence on his part.

The case was finally submitted on the 9th of April, 1874, and on the first of June, 1874, the Circuit Court made a decree restraining the defendant Chase, absolutely, "from carrying on or being directly or indirectly engaged in the business of printing or publishing in the State of Michigan, so long as Beal shall remain in or continue to carry on the business of printing and publishing in the city of Ann Arbor," and restraining the defendant corporation "from printing or publishing, or being in any manner, directly or indirectly, interested in printing or publishing in this State, 'Dr. Chase's Family Physician, Farrier, Bee-Keeper and Second Receipt Book,' so long as Beal shall contiune to carry on the printing and publishing business in Ann Arbor, and shall continue to print and publish the first book, being Dr. Chase's Recipes, or Information for Everybody,'" and

2d, restraining the company " from carrying on or continuing the business of printing or publishing within said State of Michigan, in connection with Chase, or wherein Chase shall be directly or indirectly engaged OR INTERESTED; and from printing or publishing, in connection as partners or otherwise, with said Chase, or for his benefit in whole or in part, within said State, Dr. Chase's Family Physician, &c., and Second Receipt Book, so long as Beal shall remain in the printing and publishing business, in Ann Arbor, and shall continue to print ' Dr. Chase's Recipes ;' and the injunction before granted as to the letters, as modified by the order, on page 108 of Record, was continued in force until further order, and the question of damages and costs, as well as the question of changing the injunction as to the letters and all other questions were reserved." See Record, 509 to 511. Not being able to abtain a decision of the whole case, the defendants, after waiting for that purpose until June 24th, 1874, perfected their several appeals on that day, and filed the transcript in this court, in July, 1874. On the 16th of September, 1874, the Circuit Court made its final decree, ABSOLUTELY RESTRAINING CHASE, (AND THE COMPANY ALSO, THOUGH THE COMPANY NEVER CLAIMED OR EXERCISED POSSESSION OR CONTROL OVER CHASE'S LETTERS,) FROM TAKING OR RECEIVING FROM THE POST-OFFICE IN ANN ARBOR, ANY LETTER OR LETTERS THAT MAY BE RECEIVED AT THAT OFFICE, ADDRESSED TO SAID CHASE, WHICH SHALL NOT HAVE UPON THEM A DESIGNATION OF THE NUMBER OF SAID CHASE'S PRIVATE LETTER BOX, AT SAID OFFICE, OR IN ANY MANNER INTERFERING TO PREVENT THE DELIVERY OF THE SAME TO SAID BEAL, AT SAID POST-OFFICE, AND FROM APPROPRIATING TO HIS OR THEIR USE, ANY SUCH LETTERS, OR ANY INFORMATION THEREIN CONTAINED, OR ANY MONEY, DRAFTS, OR POST-OFFICE MONEY ORDERS TRANSMITTED IN OR WITH ANY SUCH LETTER, SO LONG AS THE COMPLAINANT SHALL CONTINUE IN THE BUSINESS OF PRINTING AND PUBLISHING IN ANN ARBOR, AND REQUIRING CHASE AND THE COMPANY TO PAY TO BEAL TEN THOUSAND THREE HUNDRD AND SIXTEEN DOLLARS AND THIRTY-SIX CENTS for damages of complainant since the making of said contract, and prior to the commencement of this suit, in consequence of the carrying on by said defendants of the printing and publishing business in the city of Ann Arbor aforesaid, &c.; and also the complainant's costs of this suit, awarding execution against both defendants therefor..

From the last decree an appeal has been taken by the defendants, and though by reason of the delay in making this decree, the time required by the rule has not elapsed to entitle us to argue the last appeal, now, as matter of absolute right, we respectfully ask the court, under the circumstances of hardship in the case, to relax the rule and hear the whole case now, it being within the discretion of the court.

BRIEF AND ARGUMENT FOR THE DEFENDANTS.

I.

The contract of Chase, a citizen of Michigan, that he would not, directly or indirectly, engage in the business of printing and publishing in the State of Michigan while Beal remains in the business of printing and publishing in Ann Arbor is void, because the common law does not tolerate a contract which restrains a man from exercising his trade or useful occupation throughout the whole commonwealth, any more than it would tolerate a contract to commit suicide. That general restraints of trade and occupation extending throughout England are void, is a doctrine as old as the common law, and as firmly settled as any rule of law can be. Public policy demands, and under the free principles of the common law of England has always demanded, that the free citizen should have liberty of industry in his own occupation and calling SOMEWHERE in the State. It is unreasonable that the State should compel one of its inhabitants to choose between abandonment of occupation—compulsory idleness in the State, on one hand, or emigration from it on the other hand, as the sole alternative. No consent can give one man the right to wholly deprive the State of the public benefits of another man's industry and skill in the occupation to which he has been trained. It concerns the State that there should be no involuntary idleness within its borders, and that no man in it who is willing to work with his hand or brain should be ~~thrown~~ *driven* out of it against his will. Michigan has had, and probably still has, emigration agencies to invite settlers from abroad to her hospitable borders; but she has no agent except the self-constituted agency of this complainant to induce her people or her capital to go abroad. It is of no importance to Michigan whether a member of its population shall labor in Washtenaw, Kent or Cheboygan, but it is of the greatest importance to Michigan that there should be some spot within its broad territory where every inhabitant of the State may support himself and his family by the pursuit of his accustomed lawful avocation. A man may sell his labor, under certain limitations, but he cannot sell his idleness—he cannot bind himself to an indolence from which there is no escape but in emigration. The right to work is as undoubted and indestructable as the right to walk the earth or breathe the air. It belongs to him as a man. It cannot be abdicated or bartered away.

It is therefore well established that while a restraint of trade which covers territory less extended than the State, if founded on a valid consideration, and no more extensive or more burdensome to the party restrained than the interests of the other party reasonably and fairly requires may be lawfully contracted for, because the party restrained may carry on his business with equal advantage to himself and the public elsewhere within the commonwealth; but if the restraining contract covers the WHOLE State, then whether the State be large or small, whether the business requires a large or a small area, whether the competition would reduce the profits of the would-be monopolist or not, the courts administering the common law will look no further, but will hold the restraint absolutely void.

As long ago as the reign of Henry V., in the year 1415, it was so well settled law that a contract imposing a general restraint on trade was void, that Judge Hull flew into a passion at the very sight of such a bond, and after declaring the obligation void, and the condition contrary to the common law, he said with an oath, that if the plaintiff were present he should go to prison till he

D

paid a fine to the king. 1 Smith's Leading Cases, 648, 6th Am. Ed. And the indignation of the Judge in that case has been often commended by courts since, while disapproving of the roughness of his manner of expressing it. Smith's Contracts, 181. In fact, the making of such a contract has always been deemed an act against the public interests, approaching a misdemeanor.

In The Tailors of Ipswich vs. Shenninge, 11 Coke, Rep. 53, a., it was resolved that "at common law no one can be prohibited from working at any lawful trade, "for the law abhors idleness."

In the case of Monopolies, 11 Coke Rep., 86, " it was resolved per *totam curiam*, that a grant to the plaintiff of the sole making of cards within the realm was utterly void for two reasons: 1. That it is a monopoly and against the common law. * * * " Against the common law for four reasons: 1. All trades, as well mechanical as others, which prevent idleness, (the bane of the commonwealth,) and exercise men and youth in labor for the maintainance of themselves and their families and for the increase of their substance to serve the queen when occasion shall require, are profitable for the commonwealth." * * * " And the common law, in this point, agrees with the law of God, that every man's trade maintains his life, and therefore he ought not to be deprived or dispossessed of it, no more than his life." 3 Reeves' History of English Law, 594 to 596, Finlason's Ed., note a.

In the leading case of Mitchel vs. Reynolds, 1 Peere Williams, 181, (also found in Smith's Leading Cases,) the whole subject was carefully considered in a luminous opinion which has been referred to in every subsequent case. It was held in that case that "general restraints by agreement of parties are all void, whether by bond, covenant or promise, with or without consideration, and whether it be of the party's own trade or not," but that " a man may, upon a valuable consideration, by his own consent and for his own benefit, give over his trade and part with it to another in a particular place." And the following propositions were laid down—(the action being debt on bond.)

" 1st.—That to obtain the sole exercise of any known trade

THROUGHOUT ENGLAND is a complete monopoly, and against the policy of the law.

2d.—That when restricted to particular persons or places, (if lawfully obtained,) the same is not a monopoly.

7th.—That no man can contract not to use his trade at all.

8th.—That a partial restraint is not good without just reason and consideration."

> Mitchel vs. Reynolds, 1 Smith's Leading Cases, part 2, page 643. (Marginal paging 510, 511.)

Again in the same case, on page 646, it is said " a contract not to trade in any part of England, though with consideration, is void, for there is something more than a presumption against it, because it can never be useful to any man to restrain another from trading in all places, though it may be to restrain him from trading in some, unless he intends a monopoly, which is a crime."

In Homer vs. Ashford, 3 Bingham, 322, (in 11 English Common Law Reports,) the Court of Common Pleas, by Chief Justice Best, said : " The first object of the law is to promote the public interest ; the second to preserve the rights of individuals. The law will not permit anyone to restrain a person from doing what the public welfare and his own interest requires that he should do. Any deed, therefore, by which a person binds himself not to employ his talents, his industry, or his capital in any useful undertaking in the kingdom, would be void, because no good reason can be imagined for any person imposing such a restriction upon himself." In 2 Williams' Saunders, 156, note 1, the rule is laid down thus : " A bond, covenant or promise, even on good consideration, not to use a trade ANYWHERE IN ENGLAND, is void, as being too general a restraint of trade."

In Noble vs. Bates, 7 Cowen, 307, the court said : " A bond or promise upon good consideration not to exercise a trade for a limited time, and at a particular place, or within a particular parish, is good. But when it is general not to exercise a trade throughout the kingdom, it is bad, though founded on good consideration, as being a too unlimited restraint of trade ; and operating oppressively on one party without being of any benefit to either."

In Chappell vs. Brockway, 21 Wendell, 159, Judge Bronson said : " The common law will not permit individuals to oblige themselves by a contract when the thing to be done or omitted is injurious to the public." * * * " Contracts which go to the total restraint of trade, as that a man will not pursue his occupation or carry on business ANYWHERE IN THE STATE are void, upon whatever consideration they may be made. THEY MUST BE INJURIOUS TO THE PUBLIC, and no good reason can be shown why one individual should thus fetter himself, or another individual should contract for the restraint."

In Lawrence vs. Kidder, 10 Barbour, 647, the court by Judge Selden say: "That contracts in restraint of trade, WHICH EMBRACE THE ENTIRE KINGDOM OR STATE, are void, is a doctrine coeval with the common law. It makes no difference whether the contract is or is not limited in respect of time, whether the restraint be for one month or for life, if it be general and unlimited with respect to space, the contract is absolutely void, and no circumstances whatever can justify or uphold it." Again on page 649, " While contracts which thus go to the restraint of trade THROUGHOUT AN ENTIRE STATE OR COUNTRY are uniformly void, those which impose restraint upon it only in a particular town or district are sometimes held valid." And on page 653, of same case: " The next question is, whether in passing upon contracts of this description, we are to confine our view to our own State, or whether we are to look at the whole United States, as constituting a single State or Nation. In other words, whether the same rules are to be applied to a contract embracing the State of New York alone, as by the common law has always been applied to those embraceing the whole territory of Great Britain.

This question involves a variety of considerations, and admits, perhaps, of considerable discussion. But there are one or two leading ideas which, in my view, are decisive of it. In the first place, the people of this State have no control over, or influence upon, the municipal laws of other States. They may, if they please, impose the most burdensome restrictions upon particular trades. We cannot say, therefore, that a restraint which is co-extensive with this State leaves the residue of the Union open to the party to pursue, unrestrained, the same trade. Again: it is repugnant to the general frame and policy of our government to regard the Union, in respect to our ordinary internal and domestic interests, as one consolidated nation. For all these purposes each State is a separate community with separate and independent public interests. It is by no means the same thing to the people of this State, whether an individual carries on his trade within or without its borders. I am, therefore, of the opinion, independent of authority, that a contract prohibiting to an individual the pursuit of any trade or employment throughout the State of New York, should be regarded in total restraint of trade within the rule of the common law."

In Van Marter vs. Babcock, 23 Barbour, 636, it was said: "It is of no consequence to the public where a man carries on his trade or occupation within the State, provided he is not prohibited from doing so at all," &c.

In Dunlap vs. Gregory, 10 New York, 244, it was held that "contracts, upon whatever consideration made, which go to the total constraint of trade, such as obligate a man not to pursue his occupation or exercise his trade ANYWHERE IN THE STATE, are void."

In Taylor vs. Blanchard, 13 Allen, 370, decided in 1866, the plaintiff and defendant entered into co-partnership in the art, trade and business of manufacturing and selling shoe-cutters and all things thereto belonging, for one year, and as much longer as they should agree. The co-partnership articles contained a covenant on the part of Blanchard that at whatever time the partnership should be ended, "he, the said Blanchard, shall not, nor will not, at any time or times hereafter, either alone or jointly, with or as agent for any person whomsoever, set up or exercise, or carry on the said business of manufacturing and selling shoe-cutters at any place within the aforesaid commonwealth of Massachusetts." It appeared in the case that the manufacture of shoe-cutters is an art which can only be carried on by persons instructed in the same, and that at the date of the agreement the plaintiff had been for many years engaged in that business in Massachusetts, and that the business was then confined to the plaintiff and three other persons; that the plaintiff was then doing a large and profitable business in such manufacture and sale, and that the defendant was wholly ignorant of the business.

The court, after stating that the law had always regarded monopolies as hostile to the rights and interests of the public, and that one method for the establishment of monopolies was by private contracts in which one of the parties agreed not to engage in some specified business, proceeded as follows: "The plaintiff contends that in this country a restraint ought not to be held void unless it extends throughout the United States, because they are one country in respect to trade and business. But we cannot regard this view as just. A MONOPOLY EXTENDING THROUGHOUT THE STATE MAY BE AS REALLY INJURIOUS TO THE PEOPLE OF THE STATE AS IF IT EXTENDED THROUGHOUT THE WHOLE COUNTRY. * * * The plaintiff also contends that the ristriction in this case is reasonable, because the territory of Massachusetts is comparatively small, and the business is the manufacture of an article used only by manufacturers of shoes. BUT WE DO NOT THINK THAT THE EXTENT OF TERRITORY EMBRACED IN A STATE AFFECTS THE PRINCIPLE. WHATEVER MAY BE THE EXTENT OF THE STATE, THE MONOPOLY RESTRICTS THE CITIZEN FROM PURSUING HIS BUSINESS, UNLESS HE TRANSFERS HIS RESIDENCE AND HIS ALLEGIANCE TO SOME OTHER STATE OR COUNTRY. Its tendency is to drive business and citizens who are skilled in business from this State to other States. If one is not at liberty to carry on his business here, but is at liberty to do so elsewhere, he will be likely to go elsewhere, and employ others to go with him." And therefore the court held the contract void.

The considerations of public policy in such cases are well presented by Judge Morton, in Alger vs. Thatcher, 19 Pick., 54, a case which appears to have been elaborately argued by counsel and much considered by the court.

In Lange vs. Werk, 2 Ohio State Rep., 519, 528, (which the learned editors of Smith's Leading Cases call a leading American case on the subject, (1 Smith's Leading Cases, 658,) the court say, after a review of the cases: "These cases fully justify the conclusion that a contract in restraint of trade can only be enforced when it is made to appear from the pleadings and proofs, 1st, that the restraint is partial; 2d, that it is founded upon a valuable consideration; and 3d, that it is reasonable and not oppressive. In respect to the LAST of these requisites, Chief Justice Tindal, in Horner vs. Graves, says: " we cannot see how a better test can be applied to the question, whether reasonable or not, than by considering whether the restraint is such only as to afford a fair protection to the interests of the party in whose favor it is given, and not so large as to interfere with the interests of the public. Whatever restraint is larger than the necessary protection of the party can be of no benefit to either; it can only be oppression, and if oppression, it is, in the eye of the law, unreasonable. Whatever is injurious to the public is void, on the ground of public policy.'" And on page 530—531, the Supreme Court of Ohio further says: " No case is to be found where such a contract has been upheld which covered the whole of England or a State of this Union."

In Bowser vs. Bliss, 7 Blackford, 346, the Supreme Court of Indiana say: "There is this distinction on this subject: when the contract is for the general restraint of any business it is illegal; but it is otherwise if the restraint be partial and reasonable."

In California it is also held that a contract restraining a party from carrying on his business in the State is void, as against public policy.

Wright vs. Ryder, 36 California, 357.

More vs. Bonnet, 40 California, 251.

In the case of the Oregon Steam Navigation Company vs. Winsor, decided at the last term of the Supreme Court of the United States, and reported in vol. 6, Chicago Legal News, 357, (and in 18th Wallace, probably,) Judge Bradley said: "A contract, even on good consideration, not to use a trade anywhere in England, is held void in that country; and he adds, that the application of the rule that a general restraint of trade is void, is more difficult than a clear understanding of it, and that in this country, especially, where State lines interpose such a slight barrier to social and business intercourse, it is often difficult to decide whether a contract not to exercise a trade in a particular State, is, or is not within the rule. It has been generally held to be so." He says, "on the ground that it would compel a man thus bound to transfer his residence and allegiance to another State in order to pursue his avocation." Judge Bradley then proceeds to say that this mode of applying the rule must be received with some caution; that this is substantially one country in matters of trade and business, and that cases may arise in which it would involve too narrow a view of the subject to condemn as invalid a contract not to carry on a particular business within a particular State. He then supposes a case of two partners engaged in the manufacture of a certain article by a secret process, and afterwards separating under a contract that one of them shall not sell the manufactured article in Massachusetts, where the other resides and does business, and that the latter shall not sell the article in New York where his associate is to reside and carry on business: and asks: "Can there be any doubt that such a contract would be valid?" We answer the question—no. But why would it be valid? Because, in the first place, the contract supposed, relates to a secret, which is a well-understood exception to the rule on the subject of restraints. Bryson vs. Whitehead, 1 Simons & Stuart, 74. Morrison vs. Moat, 9 Hare, 241, 6 Eng. L & Eq., 14. Taylor vs. Blanchard, 13 Allen, 374, 2 Story Eq. Juris., sec. 952. Morrison vs. Moat, 9 Eng. L. and Eq., 182. Hard vs. Seeley, 47 Barb., 428, 434. And because, in the second place, the case put contemplates a partnership dissolution and partition, and that each party should continue to carry on his business freely, in the State of his chosen residence; and that therefore the caution to which the Judge refers has been duly observed in the decisions, without breaking down or impairing the rule for which we contend.

On referring to the facts on which the court was called to adjudicate in the case last mentioned, it is difficult to see how any question under the law, as to restraints of trade was properly in the case. It appeared that the California Steam Navigation Company, a California corporation, "engaged in navigating the waters of California, sold to the plaintiff, (which was an Oregon corporation, engaged in the like business on the Columbia river and its branches,) the steamer "New World," and took from the plaintiff a contract that the plaintiff, "the Oregon Company,) should not run or employ, or suffer to be run or employed, the said steamer, on any of the waters of the State of *California* for ten years; and subsequently the Oregon Company sold the same steamer to the defendants, and took from them a contract that it should not be run on any of the waters of the State of California, or the Columbia river and its tributaries for ten years. At the time of these sales and contracts the California company was engaged in navigating California waters exclusively, and the Oregon Company was in like manner engaged exclusively in navigating the Columbia and its branches, and at the time of the contract "the defendants were engaged in navigating the waters of Puget Sound, and WERE IN NO WISE ENGAGED in the navigation of the waters of Oregon or California, or of any of the waters described in the stipulation"

It will be observed that the contract did not restrain the seller at all; that it did not restrain the buyers from navigating any waters whatever, with as many vessels as they pleased, (except the single steamboat purchased;) and as to that boat, there was no restraint whatever in the places where the buyers were conducting their business, but only where they were not. In the language of Judge Bradley, referring to the first contract: "It involved no transfer of residence or allegiance on the part of the vendee in order to pursue its employment, nor any cessation or diminution of its business whatever." And as to the contract between the plaintiff and the defendants, Judge Bradley said: "The stipulation stands on the same ground and reason as did the first stipulation between the California and Oregon Companies."

In other words, the restraint was not upon the purchasers personally, in their business, but rather against the use by the purchasers of the steamboat, in a new business, in another state. The reasons on which the rule as to restraints are chiefly founded of course had no application to such a case. If Beal had been a resident of Texas, and in the printing business there, and had purchased these printing presses of Chase, a resident of Michigan, and had agreed with Chase that he would not use the identical presses in Michigan, there would have been no interference with occupation, and no necessity for a change of residence to another state, in order to carry on the business of the obligated party; and each state would have continued to have as fully as before the contract, the unfettered industry of its own citizens. So, if Chase had in the case last supposed covenanted not to engage in the printing business in Texas, it would not have restrained him from his occupation in Michigan, nor would it have been a general restraint within the rule for which we contend.

Smith, in his valuable work on Contracts, page 210, says that a covenant or promise not to carry on a trade within the limits of England is totally void.

Story says: "The known and established distinction is between such bargains and contracts as are in general restraint of trade, and such as are in restraint of it only as to particular places or persons, * * *. The former are universally prohibited"—1 Story, Eq., Juris., 292.

It being agreed that the common law declares a contract restraining an Englishman from pursuing his accustomed occupation within the limits of *England* to be void, I submit that there are as strong if not stronger reasons for applying the same rule to each of the states in this country. England is only a political division of the "United Kingdom of Great Britain and Ireland." It is a very small part in territorial extent of the British Empire. England, Scotland, Ireland, and Wales, to say nothing of vast colonial possessions which are by the theory of the British Government subject to a single executive and a single parliament. This consolidated legislative body has plenary legislative powers, but with us, each state has its own separate legislature, executive, and judiciary, while the Congress has very limited powers in matters of domestic and internal legislation within a state. These belong to the several states. The law which governs the validity of contracts, which regulates commercial papers and business transactions generally; which guards and regulates the domestic relations and the rights of persons, which determines the rules of descent and fixes the tenure of lands; the law under which property is acquired, protected, and transmitted is almost entirely state law. Is it claimed that the United States Congress has any power of legislation over the subject of restraining contracts (like the one here in controversy), between citizens of the same state and intended to operate only within that state? Can Congress regulate the internal trade or commerce of a state? Is it doubted that in the absence of prohibitions in state constitutions, it is within the legislative power of each state to alter or abolish the common law on this subject, and to make general restraints hereafter lawful, or to make partial as well as general restraints of trade hereafter unlawful? I submit whether this contract is an unlawful restraint of occupation belongs to state and not to national jurisprudence.

Each state has, and lawfully may have, its own internal policy for the encouragement of industry within it, and for the protection of its citizens against improvident bargains, as well as against the rapacity or greed of other citizens. A State may lawfully and properly, by its public policy, subject of course to constitutional restrictions, if any, make itself, or strive to make itself, a more desirable residence and place of business for its citizens and others, than any other State. One State may, as a matter of State policy, lawfully provide that hereafter contracts made between its citizens, less than twenty-five years of age, shall be void. Another State that all contracts allowing interest above a specified rate, shall be void. And another may provide that it shall be lawful to collect such rates of interest as the parties may have agreed to pay. The power to alter the common law resides in the legislatures of the several States and not in the national legislature in this country and this leads me to say that the common law in force in this country is State law and not United States law. The United States law is wholly constitutional and statutory except so far as the Federal Courts administer the laws of the States. In Wheaton vs. Peters, 8 Peters, 658, (11 Supreme Court Decisions, 229) the Supreme Court of the United States said: "It is clear there can be no common law of the United States. The Federal Government is composed of twenty-four sovereign and independent States; each of which may have its local usages, customs, and common law. There is no principle which pervades the Union and has the authority of law that is not embodied in the constitution or laws of the Union. The common law could be made a part of our Federal system only by legislative adoption. When, therefore, a common law right is asserted, we must look to the State where the controversy originated." And Judge McLean, sitting in Michigan, said, in Loomis vs. Clarke, 2 McLean, 572: "There is no unwritten or common law of the Union. This rule of action is found in the different States."

In the earlier case of United States vs. Hudson, 7, Cranch, 34, the Court had decided that all exercise of criminal jurisdiction in common law cases is not within the implied powers of the courts of the United States.

The Judge in the court below seems to have thought that though the common law on this subject of restraints by contract as found in the "older reports," would render the contract void, it had been modified by the courts by recent decisions, (Record, 93) but he failed to point to the decisions which would accomplish such a result. The common law is in force here as in some sort of an inheritance of the people of the State of Michigan, and because it has been recognized by the legislature and the courts from the beginning, and because the constitutions of the State have adopted it. The present constitution provides that " the COMMON LAW and the statute laws now in force, not repugnant to this constitution, shall remain in force until they expire by their own limitation, or are altered or repealed by the legislature." Schedule, Section 1. 2 Douglass, 184, 189. The common law here is as completely State law as are the State statutes.

Complainant's counsel will concede that a general restraint is void. Can there be any doubt that WITHIN THE MEANING OF A STATE LAW a restraint which covers the whole State is A GENERAL RESTRAINT? Are the courts of Michigan to construe a contract between citizens of this State which restrains one of them from pursuing his occupation and trade, at all, in Michigan, as only a limited and partial restraint within the meaning of the laws of Michigan?

In the United States vs. DeWitt, 9 Wallace, 41, 43, 44, the Court said in 1869 : " The questions certified resolve themselves into this : Has Congress power under the constitution to prohibit trade within the limits of a State ? That Congress has power to regulate commerce with foreign nations and among the several States, and with Indian tribes, the constitution expressly declares. But this express grant of power has always been understood as limited by its terms ; and as a virtual denial of any power to interfere with the internal trade and business of the separate States ; except indeed as a necessary and proper means for carrying into execution some other power power expressly granted."

I conclude then, that the question in this case is a State question, and to be determined by considerations applicable to Michigan alone. In this case it might have been competent for Chase to have agreed with Beal that he would not infringe the copyrights sold within the State of Michigan, or within the United States, (because monopolies in copyrights and patents are secured to the owners,) though such a contract would have been entirely useless under the copyright laws. It might have been competent to agree not to pursue his business in Texas or Japan, if Beal's interests and the circumstances of the contract rendered such a restriction reasonable and fair. But I submit that subject to the exceptions stated, (including the case of the sale of a secret) a contract restraining a party from pursuing his accustomed occupation in his own State is utterly and under all circumstances void.

In the case of Whittaker vs. Howe, 3 Beavan, 383, decided in 1841, the Master of the Rolls held that an agreement by a solicitor in consideration of five thousand pounds not to practice as solicitor or attorney for twenty years in any part of Great Britain is valid. Not only does that case seem to be destitute of precedent authority for its support, but it is against the uniform language of all the other books. I cannot find that it has ever been followed or cited with approbation by any Court or Judge. In 1 Smith's Leading Cases, 649, (sixth American edition, marginal page 516,) that learned and accurate writer said: "The case goes further than any other, and its correctness may, perhaps, be questioned." Mr. Kerr, in his excellent book on Injunctions, page 508, says that the case of Whittaker vs. Howe, cannot be considered sound law. It is quite inconsistent with Ward vs. Byrnh, 5 Meeson & Welsby, 548, which was decided after mature deliberation.

In 1847, in Nicholls vs. Stretton, 10 Adolphus & Ellis, new series, 346, 353, one of the counsel referred to Whittaker vs. Howe, on the argument, but Judge Patteson said he did not see how the case of Ward vs. Byrne could be reconciled with that case. Ward vs. Byrne having been decided in Exchequer Chamber, is a case of the highest authority.

Whittaker vs. Howe is very properly placed by Redfield in the list of overruled and doubted cases. Redfield's Overruled Cases, 540. He refers to the note to Tallis vs. Tallis, 16 Juris., 744, 746, (1852,) to which I have not had access.

It seems difficult to maintain the decision in Whittaker vs. Howe without a total abandonment of the rule as to general restraints, (except on the theory that the practice of the law is not one of the useful occupations!) On that distinction in Harrison vs. Lockhart, 25 Indiana, 112, it was held that a contract not to engage in the sale of intoxicating liquors was valid.

There are these further differences between Whittaker vs. Howe and this case: The occupation of an attorney and solicitor takes a larger territory than almost any other business, and in Whittaker vs. Howe the consideration for the restraint was large, ($25,000,) while here it was nothing.

Before leaving this branch of the case it is proper to suggest that the cases in which the test of validity has been declared by the courts to be: Is the restraint considering the circumstances, fair and reasonable, and no more than the protection of the obligee or promisee requires, and is it founded on a valuable consideration?—have been cases of limited restraint; and that the application of such a test as the sole one to such cases does not at all impugn the proposition that a restraint covering the whole State is *ipso facto* void.

II.

The covenant not to engage in the printing and publishing business in Michigan is void even under the law as to limited restraints, because it is unreasonable as between the parties, and is broader and more burdensome to Chase than is necessary for the fair protection of Beal.

Hubbard vs. Miller, 27, Michigan, 20, 23.

In Horner vs. Graves, 7 Bingham, 743, decided in 1831, (same case 20 Eng. Com. Law Rep., 330,) the defendant who was a dentist, contracted not to carry on the business of his profession within one hundred miles of the city of York. Chief Justice Tindall in giving the judgment of the Court arresting judgment on the ground that the contract was void, said: "We do not see how a better test can be applied to the question than by considering whether the restraint is such ONLY as to afford a fair protection to the interest of the party in favor of whom it is given, and not so large as to interfere with the interests of the public. Whatever restraint is larger than the NECESSARY protection of the party, can be of no benefit to either; it can only be oppressive, and if oppressive, it is, in the eye of the law, unreasonable. Whatever is injurious to the interests of the public is void on the ground of public policy."

In Hitchcock vs. Coker, 6 Adolphus & Ellis, 438, 443, (33 Eng. Com. Law, 241, 244,) decided in 1837, the contract was that defendant would not directly or indirectly carry on the business of a chemist or druggist in the town of Taunton, or within three miles thereof. Erle appeared as one of the counsel for defendant. Chief Justice Denman in giving the judgment of the court of King's Bench holding the contract void after stating that " the law upon this subject has been settled by a series of decisions that an agreement for a partial and reasonable restraint of trade upon an adequate consideration is binding, but that an agreement for general restraint is illegal;" and after referring to Horner vs. Graves, said: " It appears quite safe to hold that the law will not enforce any agreement for curtailing the rights both of the public and the contracting party, without it be necessary for the protection of him in whose favor it was made," On error in the same case in the Exchequer Chamber the Court agreed to the principle laid down in the King's Bench, but held that in the particular case the restraint was not in point of fact unreasonable in extent.

 See also, Mallan vs. May, 11 Meeson & Welsby, 652, 666, 667.

 Avery vs. Langford, Kay, 663.

 Allsopp vs. Wheatcraft, Law Rep., 15 Eq. Cases, 59. Same case, 5 Eng. Rep. by Moak, 714, 718, 719.

In Gale vs. Reed, 8 East, 86, Lord Ellenborough said: " The restraint on one side meant to be enforced should in reason be coextensive only with the benefits meant to be enjoyed on the other."

 Young vs. Timmins, 1 Cromp. & Jervis, 331, 340, 343.

Ward vs. Byrne, 5 Meeson & Welsby, 547, 558, 559, 561, 562.
Mitchell vs. Reynolds, 1 Peere Williams, 181.
Lange vs. Werk, 2 Ohio St. Rep., 519.
Grasselli vs. Lowden, 11 Ohio St. Rep., 349.
Crawford vs. Wick, 18 Ohio St. Rep., 190.
Nobles vs. Bates, 7 Cawen, 309.
Chappel vs. Brockway, 21 Wend, 158.
Ross vs. Sedgbeer, 21 Wend, 165.
Hooker vs. Vandewater, 4 Denio, 349.
Stanton vs. Allen, 4 Denio, 434.
Lawrence vs. Kidder, 10 Barbour, 641, 649, 651, 552.
Mott vs. Mott, 11 Barbour, 127.
Holbrook vs. Waters, 9 Howard, Pr. Rep. ~~355.~~
Dunlop vs. Gregory, 10 N. Y., 241, 244.
Keeler vs. Taylor, 53 Pa. St., 468, 469.
McClurg's Appeal, 58 Pa. St., 51.
Guerand vs. Dandelett, 32 Md., 561. Same case, 3d American Rep., 164, 167.
Brewer vs. Marshall, 4 Green, (N. J.,) 537.
~~Geunther vs. Dewin, 11 Iowa, 133.~~
~~Reynolds vs. Nichols, 12 Iowa, 399.~~
Kellogg vs. Larkin, 3 Chandler, (Wis.,) 133.
Holmes vs. Martin, 10 Ga., 503.
Beard vs. Dennis, 6 Ind., 204.

In Mallan vs. May, 11 Meeson & Welsby 653, 666, the language of Chief Justice Tindal in Homer vs Graves, above quoted, was re affirmed in 1843. In that case the covenants were twofold, 1st, That the defendant whom the plaintiffs took into their service as assistant in the business of surgeon dentists, for four years, would not after the expiration of that time carry on that business in London, and 2nd, That the defendant would not carry on that business in any of the towns of England or Scotland, where the plaintiff might have been practicing before the expiration of that term. The Court held the covenant good as to London, but that the covenant restraining the defendant from practicing in any of the towns of England or Scotland, where the plaintiffs might have been practicing, was void. The Court said: "This covenant goes much beyond what the protection of any interests of the plaintiffs could reasonably require, and puts into their hands the power of preventing the defendant from practicing anywhere. We are therefore of the opinion that it is an unreasonable restriction, and that the defendant is entitled to our judgment on the demurer on the second breach."

The Court of Appeals of New York, in Dunlap vs Gregory, said: "The contract, to be upheld, must appear from special circumstances to be reasonable, and useful, and THE RESTRAINT OF THE COVENANTOR MUST NOT BE LARGER THAN IS NECESSARY FOR THE PROTECTION OF THE COVENANTEE IN THE ENJOYMENT OF HIS TRADE OR BUSINESS," 10 N. Y., 244.

In Morse Twist Drill and Machine Co. vs Morse, 103 Mass, 73, 74, 75, the defendant in order to induce the organization of the company, sold to the plaintiff two patents, which had been issued to him, and agreed to transfer to them all improvements, new modes of manufacture, and inventions relating to the subject matter of the patents, which he might make or invent, and that he would use his best efforts for the prefecting of improvements in the business and manufacture; and covenanted that he would do no act that might injure the company or its business, and that he would at no time aid, assist, or encourage any competition against the Company. The defendant also agreed to give his whole time to the Company for three years, The consideration for these assignments and covenants was ten thousand dollars, and $1,500 per year.

The Court expresly affirmed the decision in Taylor & Blanchard, 13 Allen, 370, and said that the question was whether the rule laid down in that case extended to a case like the one in the Morse case, and then proceeded to say that the rule, as to restraints, had never been extended to a business practiced by a patent, or to a business which is a secret not known to the public, because the public had no rights in such a case. Those considerations of course disposed of all questions touching the validity of the contract, except the part wherein the defendant covenanted that he would do nothing to the injury of the company, and that he would not assist or encourage competition against the company.

G

The case might well have have beeen disposed of on the principles applicable to patents and secrets, as those were the foundation subjects of the contract, to which all the rest was merely incidental. But there is nothing in that case which sustains the contract in this.

In the Morse case the restraint was carefully bounded by the limits of the vendee's interests under the purchase. It could not be said in that case that the restraint was broader than the vendor's protection required. It was so expressly limited in its terms that it could not possibly extend beyond such protection. The restraint did not compel the defendant to abandon his trade or calling as an inventor and machinist. It only restricted him from competing in the manufacture of one specific article. It left open to him the whole field of mechanics and mechanism besides. It was as if a druggist, having compounded a drug, supposed to possess medicinal value, should sell his stock to another, and agree not to compete with the purchaser in the sale of that drug. The vendor could still pursue his occupation as a druggist, and sell every other article known in the *Materia Medica*, and the chief reasons on which the rule for which we contend is founded, would not exist in such a case. It would be a case of limited and partial restraint only, and with no POSSIBILITY of needless and useless oppression. The public would still have the benefit of the industry and skill of the citizens in his accustomed occupation. In other words it would be a LIMITED restraint, not taking the covenantor out of his calling, and not greater than was necessary for the protection of the covenantee; and it matters not, perhaps, whether such a limitation be accomplished by territorial bounds, or by any other, so long as the covenantor's right to pursue his general calling in the State, and the public interests are protected from invasion.

The cases referred to in 103 Mass. 76, from the Weekly Reporter and The Jurist, are not found in the regular reports, and therefore I have not seen them; but it is apparent from the statement of them in the Massachusetts case that the restraints were limited in character, and did not drive the parties from their principal calling. So that whether those cases were rightly decided or not, they are distinguishable from Chase's case, by the two important facts, 1st, that in each of those cases the restraint was strictly limited to the prevention of competition, with the single subject matter of the sale—limited to the needed protection of the purchaser ; and 2nd, that in each of them the covenantor was left at liberty to pursue his principal business. For instance, in Ainsworth vs. Bentley, the defendant, a general publisher, agreed that he would not publish another periodical of the same character as "Bentley's Miscellany." If he had agreed not to publish anything whatever, the case would have been parallel. But the whole domain of printing was left open to him, except the publication of a magazine, like "Bentley's Miscellany."

The following cases were restraints as to secrets, which, as before stated, are exceptions to the rule:

 Bryson vs. Whitehead, 1 Sim, and Stuart, 74.
 Morrison vs Moat, 9 Hare, 241.
 Same case, 6 English, L & Eq., 14, and
  11 English L. & Eq., 182.
 Leather Cloth Co. vs. Lorsont, Law Rep., 9 Eq, 345, 354.
 Vickery vs. Welch, 19 Pick., 523.
 Peabody vs. Norfolk, 98 Mass., 452, 459, 460.
 Jarvis vs. Peck, 10 Paige, 118.
 Alcock vs. Giberton, 5 Duer, 76.
 Hart vs. Seeley, 47 Barb., 428.

In Leather Cloth Co. vs. Lorsont, the Vice Chancellor, on page 354, says: "Now, in this case, the subject matter of the contract was a particular manufacture carried on, partly under patents and partly by processes, which it is to be assumed were not known except to the vendors themselves, and their agents and workmen. THAT BEING THE SUBJECT MATTER OF THE CONTRACT, the stipulation is, that the vendors will not set up a similar manufacture in Europe, and will not communicate the process of the manufacture anywhere, so as to interfere with the enjoyment by the intended company, of the benefits thereby agreed to be purchased. This case, as it seems to me, much more resembles the sale of a SECRET, which has been held to be perfectly good, with a stipulation unlimited as to time and place, as to communicating the secret or dealing with it so as to interfere with the purchaser. It is settled by authority that a man may bind himself not to communicate that process to anybody else, anywhere, under any circumstances, in any part of the world." And on THAT GROUND the Vice Chancellor supported the contract. It is apparent that it could not have been supported on any other ground, without overturning the decisions of all the Common Law Judges in Exchequer Chamber on a common law question. There are, no doubt, *dicta* in the opinion of the Vice Chancellor, which it is difficult to reconcile with the other cases, unless limited to the case of a secret, which was, in fact, the ONLY case before the Court.

In Allsopp vs. Wheatcraft, 15 Eq. cases, 59, 64, 65, decided in 1872, the defendant had entered into the service of the plaintiffs (the plaintiffs being brewers, at Burton,) under a contract whereby he agreed that he would not at any time during his said service, or within two years after quitting the plaintiff's service, either directly or indirectly sell, procure orders for the sale, or recommend, or be in anywise concerned or engaged in the sale or recommendation of any Burton ale, or beer, or porter, or any brewed at that place, or any offered for sale as such, other than the ale, beer or porter brewed by the plaintiffs. After remaining in the service of plaintiffs for five years the defendant left them and violated the terms of his contract by entering the service of other brewers at Burton and soliciting orders for other ales than plaintiffs'. Vice Chancellor Wickens refused to grant an injunction, and held the contract void. He declined to adopt the *dicta* in Leather Cloth Co. vs. Lorsont as applicable to such a case, and explained that there were expressions in the contract in Leather Cloth Co. case limiting the generality of the contract, and that it was, in substance, a case of a different class from Allsop vs. Wheatcroft, since the restriction against trading in the former case was only a consequence of a clearly lawful restriction against divulging a secret.

It was argued in Allsopp vs. Wheatcroft that under the covenant the defendant could not act as a beer merchant, beer bottler, a cellarman, publican, barman or waiter; that such a sweeping restraint was not necessary for the plaintiff's protection, and that the covenant was therefore unreasonable and void, independent of considerations of space. The Vice Chancellor sustained that view by his judgment in the case. He also held that the restraint was too general as to space.

The principles of that decision are fatal to this covenant which prohibits Chase from engaging in the printing and publishing business, directly or indirectly, in the State of Michigan, &c. That is to say, he cannot be type-setter, proofreader, folder, pressman, or engineer. He cannot act in the most trivial or subordinate positions. He could not act as a newsboy on the streets. He is prohibited from starting a weekly newspaper or using a handpress, or doing the smallest job of printing in the most obscure town or in the most remote or isolated part of the State, though Mr. Beal or his printing establishment had never been dreamed of there. He cannot go to Marquette or Shanty Plains and set up the types for a hand-bill, " directly or indirectly." According to the decree in this case, he cannot own a dollar's worth of stock in a printing company anywhere in the State, though he may give the business no personal attention whatever, or even sell his own manuscript works to others and take his compensation in the ordinary way of royalty. He cannot set type for a book in Hebrew or Sanscrit, or in any department of printing, though Beal may not be able or may not undertake to do such work at all, and though there may be no possibility of injury to Beal from Chase's doing it. Will it be said that a restraint so sweeping and despotic as this, is necessary for the fair and reasonable protection of Beal in the matter of his purchase? It surely is not, whether we look at the extent of territory covered by it or at the generality of the restraint itself without reference to space. The restraint is oppressive and unreasonable, and the covenant being entire, it is therefore wholly void. If the covenant had been sufficiently limited in its nature and had extended to the county of Washtenaw, or the State divisibly, it might, under the authority of some of the cases, be so divided and held good as to one territory, though void as to the other. (Though, on this point, More vs. Bonnett, 40 California, 251, seems based on the better reason.) But there is only one territory designated in this contract, and that is the State of Michigan. It is good for the whole State, or for no part of it. To hold otherwise would make a new contract for the parties which they never made themselves.

H

When we look at the facts of this case the unreasonableness of the covenant is still more apparent than when we consider it abstractly.

The case made by the bill is that it was the intention of the contract to restrain Chase altogether from engaging in the printing business again. The bill goes even further and alleges distinctly that Chase " assured your orator and AGREED with him that upon said sale being made he WOULD RETIRE ALTOGETHER FROM SUCH business." etc. Record, page 7.

The answer denies this: and I only refer it to show that on the complainant's allegations a sweeping general restraint was intended, such as no Judge by decisions or *dictum*, has ever said anything to sanction.

When we refer to the testimony, what, at the time of the sale, was the extent of the printing business of Dr. Chase? The answers avered that it extended to only a small portion of the State, and was chiefly in Washtenaw county. It therefore devolved on Beal, if he claims it to be more extensive, to show it by the proofs.

It cannot be supposed that the covenant was intended to prohibit Chase from printing or publishing the COPYRIGHT books he sold to Beal, because the coppright laws afforded ample protection and the best possible prohibitions against that. There is no pretence in the case of any actual or contemplated infringement of copyright. There was only the newspaper and the job printing on which such a covenant could be of value, or which could have been within the intent of the parties; and, therefore, in considering the business to be protected by the restraint, reference is to be had to the job printing and newspaper alone.

The newspaper, the Peninsular Courier and Family Visitant. was a weekly newspaper of small circulation, and that chiefly confined to Washtenaw county.

That is Chase's testimony. Record, 272, 273.

It is also the testimony of Beal:

" Question. What was the circulation of the Peninsular Courier and Visitant at the time you took possession of it?"

" Answer. I think between 1400 and 1500: my recollection of

it might be more or less than 1500. I think it was about 1500. * * *."

" Question. Where was the circulation chiefly?"

" Answer. Chiefly in Washtenaw county." Record, 186.

Beal further testified that at the time he gave his evidence, (Spring of 1874,) the circulation was not so large as when the injunction was granted, (July, 1873). See Record, 187.

So local and obscure was and is the newspaper, that Beal put in it an advertisement of a new edition of his book which he swears he was very careful to keep from the knowledge of his agents, because, as he testifies, he knew that if his agents got hold of the advertisement it might stop the sale of his book, (Record, 374) and therefore, to keep the secret perfectly secure he put the advsrtisement in his newspaper.

The job printing was a mere local business, confined chiefly to Washtenaw county, and was small in amount. The bill does not show how evtensive it was, it seeming to be the purpose of the complainant throughout the case, to conceal its amount, and to aggregate it with the sales of the copyright book.

But Chase's answer shows what its character was. (Record, page 48).

The gross amount of job work done for parties living outside of Washtenaw county from July, 1867, to April 1st, 1869, was only eighteen hundred and twelve dollars and seventy-two cents, ($1,812.72).

During the same period the work done for parties living within that county was about ten times as much, being ($18,842.80).

See testimony of Dr. Chase, Record, 273, 274.

From September 2d, 1869, to March, 1870, the total job printing done by Beal, as successor to Chase, was $8,232 98, of which only $579 18 was for parties outside Washtenaw county, Record, 403, 404. And from April 1st, 1870, to September 2d, 1870, the total job printing done by Beal was $4,686 67, of which only seventy-three dollars and fifty-five cents ($73 55) was done for parties outside Washtenaw county. Record, page 416.

And from September 2d, 1870, to June 7th, 1871, Beal's total job printing, according to his own books, was twelve thousand one hundred and seventeen dollars and ninety-three cents

($12,117 93) of which only nine hundred and fifteen dollars and ten cents ($915 10) was for parties living outside of Washtenaw county.

Record, page 401.

So that from the time of his purchase, August 30th, 1869, to June 7th 1871, during a period of more than twenty-one months, the total job printing business done by Beal, which was not Washtenaw county business, was only fifteen hundred and sixty-seven dollars and eighty-three cents ($1,567 83,) being only about seventy dollars per month ; and in the last fourteen months of that time the job printing from outside Washtenaw county, was less than fifty dollars a month, counting everything, whether collectable or not. That is to say, for the twenty-one months following Beal's purchase the printing done for parties outside Washtenaw county was only about six per cent. of job printing done at the establishment, and for the period specified before the sale the job printing not belonging to the county was less than ten per cent. And of this small amount of outside work the testimony shows that a large share was for Wayne county. Of the $1,812.-72 above mentioned $691.11 was for Detroit.

Record, page 275.

The case shows that prior to the sale to Beal, ninety per cent of the job printing was for Washtenaw county, and that scarcely anything was done for that part of the State north of the Detroit and Milwaukee Railroad or west of the meridian of Marshall.

Record, pages 48, 65, 278, 279.

No witness contradicts the figures above given by the witnesses Chase, Watson, and Messrs. Dean, showing the limited amount of job printing from without the county of Washtenaw. Beal called Mr. Clark to prove the amount of outside work from April 1st, 1869, to August 26, 1869. Record, pages 218 to 223. The aggregate for that period as stated by Clark, was $3,166.81, as appears by footing up his items, Record, 218 to 223, 226, 227, (and which items he states on page 232, were all he found,) but in that amount were included charges for work done for Beal himself, for the Diocese of Michigan, ordered by the Rev. Dr. Gillespie, of Ann Arbor; for hotel registers for Ypsilanti and Saline ; for the State Agricultural Society on the order of Gilbert, of Ypsilanti, chairman of business committee; for Agatha Kalmbach, of Ann Arbor; for Azubia Spring, then of Ann Arbor; for Messrs. Payne & Goodman, for the Michigan Teacher on the order of the member of the firm who then lived at Ypsilanti, etc. The errors pointed out by Dr. Chase's testimony show that the above amount should be reduced by seven hundred and two dollars and thirty-nine cents.

It appeared by uncontradicted testimony that of the work included in Clark's list as outside work, all the work for the Methodist conferences was done by the order of J. M. Arnold, of Detroit; that one of said Methodist conferences, for printing the proceedings of which Clark included in his list of outside work, held its session at Ann Arbor; that the work for Albion College came to Chase as a Methodist, and after a donation of one hundred dollars by him to the College, that he got the printing of the proceedings of the Odd Fellows' Grand Lodge because he was a member of the order, and the Secretary, Mr. Sprague, resided in Ann Arbor, that the Port Huron catalogues were ordered through Mr. Frazer, formerly of Ann Arbor, and whose father still lived there, that D. B. Briggs, for whom the work on the Romeo Journal was done, went from Ann Arbor; that John Davis & Co., of Chicago, for whom $6 75 worth of work was done, put in steam fixtures for Chase at Ann Arbor, and that the order from Dr. Kidder, of Evanston, Illinois, probably came because Chase was then supporting a young man at that institution being educated for the ministry. See Record, pages 275, 278. It may be mentioned that there is a discrepancy of over $200 between the true aggregate of the items stated by Clark, and the aggregate given by him on page 382.

It appears from the figures that the exact per cent of the printing business done for parties outside of Washtenaw county from July 22d, 1867, to April 1, 1869, was only eight and seventy-seven one hundredths per cent. of Chase's job printing business for that period. And that combining the Detroit business of $691.11, done within the same time with the Washtenaw county business, only five and forty-three one hundredths per cent. of Chase's job printing business was done for parties residing out of Washtenaw county or Detroit for the same period, being for one year, eight months, and nine days. Record, 274.

It also appears from the uncontradicted figures that the total job printing done by Beal from September 2d, 1869, to June 2d, 1871, was $25,037.58, (Record, 401, 403, 416,) of which amount there was done for parties residing out of Washtenaw county work to the amount of only $1,586.78 (Record, 401, 404, 426). Showing that of the entire job printing business for that period of one year, nine months, and three days, immediately succeeding the taking possession by Beal, ninety-three and sixty-six one hundredths per cent. was strictly Washtenaw county business, and only six and thirty-four one hundredths per cent. for parties outside of Washtenaw county.

It appears that the only counties in the State for residents of which any printing whatever was done by the establishment besides Washtenaw, were Livingston, pages 219, 220; Jackson, 219, 220; Monroe, 219; Lenawee, 219; Calhoun, 220, 221, 226; Oakland, 220, 221; Macomb, 220, 221, 223; Genessee, 221; Hillsdale, 221, 226; St. Clair, 221, and Wayne, 219, 222, 226, 229, 230, 275. And it will be seen that the business done for parties in most of those counties was very small, and that the whole number of counties, not encluding Washtenaw, was eleven. There were seventy-seven counties in Michigan in 1873, and in sixty-five of them, no resident inhabitant, so far as appears, ever furnished any printing business for this establishment. For some of the eleven counties above mentioned, only a single job was done, and it would be absurd, from the evidence, to consider this establishment as having continuous customers in those counties ordering printing done at that establishment.

There are in Michigan 56.451 square miles.

The twelve counties above mentioned, including Washtenaw, contain only 7,853 square miles, and therefore it appears that from the counties embracing eighty-six nine-tenths per cent. of the territory of the State, no person has ever given this establishment an order for printing.

It clearly appears from the testimony that the job printing was essentially a mere local business, (and we claim that the business of printing is, intrinsically, a mere local business).

Even if the copies of the " Recipe Book," printed at this establishment under copyright, should be taken into consideration in determining the extent of the printing business to which the restraining covenant referred, the local character of the business of printing, as done at that establishment by Chase, would not be changed. That book was printed and published at Ann Arbor, by and for Dr. Chase himself and not on the order of anybody else, and, so far as Dr. Chase was concerned, the sales of the book, (excepting those made to Bancroft, of San Francisco,) were wholly made at Ann Arbor and paid for there. The so-called agents were, in fact, purchasers of the book, who remitted to Ann Arbor payment in full before shipment by Dr. Chase.

Dr. Chase's Answer, page 33, and his testimony, pages 287, 288.

Dr. Chase, in his testimony, estimated the amount of printing done at the establishment in question at about one seventy-fifth of the printing done in the State. The correctness of this estimate was not disputed by any other witness.

The testimony of Dr. Chase also showed that sales of the first Recipe book, in Michigan, had nearly ceased before Beal's purchase—the demand having been supplied.

It being undisputed law that all restraints of trade and occupation are void if considered in the abstract, or unless under the circumstances shown they appear to be reasonable, fair and necessary for the just protection of the party for whose benefit they are made, and not unnecessarily injurious to the public, it devolved upon Beal (as having the burden of proof cast upon him) to show the necessary facts to warrant the restraint in question.

III.

The case alleged by the bill is an argreement on the part of Chase to retire altogether from the printing and publishing business. Record, page 7.

Nobody will claim such a contract to be valid. Is the complainant entitled to any decree under SUCH A BILL, whatever may be thought of the points heretofore made?

IV.

The complaintant is debarred from any relief in equity by his *laches* and his acquiescence for so long a period in the right of Chase and the company to print and publish, notwithstanding the covenant.

> Saunders vs. Smith, 3 Mylne & Craig, 711; (14 Eng. Ch., 712, 718, 730, 736).
>
> Beard vs. Turner, 13 Law Times' Rep., n. s., 747. (Also reported in Cox's Trade Mark Cases, 717).
>
> Bovill vs. Crate, Law Rep., 1 Eq., 387.
>
> Lehman vs. McArthur, Law Rep., 3 Ch. App., 496.
>
> Hilliard on Injunctions, p. 29, section 43.
>
> Kerr on Injunctions, 202, 204, 299, 349.

Chase informed Beal of his purpose to engage in the printing business about a year and a half before the organization of the company, had rented a building in Ann Arbor with that object, ordered $8,000 worth of printing material, and was at work setting type for his new receipt book. These facts were well and publicly known.

> See Record, 280.

After that the company was organized in August, 1872, and had invested $25,000 of paid up capital, had been publishing its newspaper eight or nine months, had been doing a general printing business, and had been getting out the Second Receipt Book nearly a year, and had published it about four months before the filing of this bill, without any attempt on the part of Beal to enforce this restraining covenent.

> See Record, 286, 289.

The company took possession early in August, 1872.

Chase had been preparing the Second Receipt Book for publication with full knowledge of Beal for some years before its publication.

Record, 305, 306.

It is true that in October, 1872, Beal filed a bill against the defendants to restrain the publication of the Second Receipt Book, on the ground that it was a violation of his rights under the law of Trade Marks, and that the bill alleged that Chase had made a covenant not to engage in the printing and publishing business in Michigan, but the bill sought no specific relief beyond the prevention of the publication of the book.

Record, 488 to 491.

On the argument of the motion for an injunction on that bill before Judge Higby, Mr. Pond, the counsel for Beal, waived any claim under the restraining contract and stated that they made no contest in that matter.

See testimony of Zina P. King, Record, 431.

The Ann Arbor Printing and Publishing Company contemplated the publication of a series of mathematical works and other books, and the republication of certain law books, (Record, 413,) and before the filing of this bill had expended between $27,000 and $28,000 (Record, 415). The discontinuance of the company or its business would produce a very great loss in these expenditures, (Record 304, 415, 399, 400, 409, 410.

V.

If the restraining covenant was in issue in the first suit, would not the decision of Judge Higby, denying the motion for injunction bar further litigation for its enforcement? A judgment on the faith of admissions or waivers is as conclusive on questions within the scope of the judgment and covered by it as if the result had been reached after controversy.

VI.

So far as the decision may turn (if it should turn at all,) on any question of veracity between Beal and Chase, a reference to the Record will sufficiently show which is best entitled to credit.

For Beal's exhibition of himself, see Record, 195, where, after admitting that he published, February 14th, 1873, the following statement in his newepaper: "This office has had a larger run of job work for the last four months than for any previous four months, for which we feel very thankful;" testified as follows:

"Question. Did you say that?"

"Answer. Yes, sir; I thought that was a pretty good article, too; I used to get up in the night to read it for ten days after it was out."

Though he testified to the gross receipts as shown by his books, (see page 366, 368,) and though after much equivocation, (see pages 370, 371, 386, 387, 388, 389, 390,) and after claiming that he did not know the amounts of receipts from the "Recipe Book" and "job printing" separately, he was at last obliged to confess on pages 390, 391, that there was a separate account for each, and that in order to obtain the aggregate receipts, he had in fact, added together the receipts kept separately for each branch of the business, and that the ledger and cash book would show. And on page 391, he confessed that he had made up a statement called for months before by us, (in his first testimony,) but never produced, which would show the receipts for each year of the "Receipe Book" the "job printing," &c., separately. He refused to allow Prof. Watson, Col. Dean, Sedgwick Dean, or Mr. King to determine the amount of sales for the years from August, 1869, to August, 1873, of "Dr. Chase's Recipe's" book by inspection of his books then in court, even in his own presence and in presence of the court; and in this refusal he was sustained by the Circuit Judge. Record, 386, 384, 385. The gentlemen named were experts in book-keeping. The record shows that we were unable to obtain any division of the gross receipts claimed, into the appropriate branches of the business, or to test by our own experts the correctness of the general statements made on the part of Beal.

The Circuit Judge sustained the objections of Beal's counsel to an investigation of Beal's income returns and the sources of income referred to therein, (pps. 193, 194,) though he permitted copies of the returns to be appended for consideration by this court. See Returns pp. 153 to 154, 248 to 249, 471 to 480.

The extracts from his paper put in evidence on pages 194, 195, 196, 197, are inconsistent with his claims in this suit.

Apprehending that the advertisement of a new edition of his book in his paper of February 14th, 1873, and in subsequent numbers, (Record 195,) would affect injuriously his case, he claimed that he carefully kept the fact from the knowledge of his agents.

He declined to say whether the distinguished physician referred to in his advertisement on page 196, was Vance or Briggs. (216.)

He had heard some talk about the merging of parol negotiations in the written contract, and therefore he says on page 212: " The whole thing was the parol agreement between us, and at the time, my recollection is the whole thing was a parol agreement, and everything was merged in the parol agreement," &c.

According to Beal's own testimony there was no need of the holding out to him of any inducements to buy the establishment. He seems to have seized the opportunity of Chase's convalescence from a severe illness to drive a hard bargain, not different in character from the one made in the olden time with the poor weaver, which Judge Hull so denounced. See remarks of Chief Justice Parker on the case in 2 Henry V., reported 1 Peere Williams, 193, and in 1 Smith's Leading Cases, 646, sixth American Edition, (marginal page 514.) See Record 123 to 126. Beal says that he had some talk with Chase about two years before the purchase in which Chase gave him the refusal of the property for ten days; but that at the end of the fifth day, Beal declined to take the property, and that Chase told him he was very glad of it; that from that time he (Beal) watched everything connected with the business; that he " was sorry all the while ;" that Chase " said I had made a mistake that I had not bought him out, and I thought so too; so I didn't have no long talk about it BECAUSE I SEE HE DIDN'T CARE ABOUT selling, but I kept watch of everything about the business. I calculated as soon as he got ready to sell, to buy him out."

After Chase's illness he wrote Beal about board in Minnesota and Beal concluded (so he testifies) that Chase had got ready to sell, " so I wrote him a letter and asked him what he would take for the property. At all events I found out while he was there that he wanted to sell badly AND HE MIGHT BACK OUT IN A HURRY, so I calculated I should buy him out and when I got down here I found him fever heat to sell out. I WAS JUST AS ANXIOUS TO BUY HIM OUT, SO IT DIDN'T TAKE A GREAT WHILE TO GET AT IT."

Beal's testimony, 124, 125, 126.

Again, on page 132, Beal testified respecting Chase's health: "His sight was poor, and his health failing, he was admonished, and he must close up his earthly matters; said all his relations and father had died at an early age, and he could not possibly live over fifty-six; and says I: 'You look well and ought not to die yet.' Says he: 'I ain't afraid to die; I am prepared: I am a good Christian man; all my relatives are going * * * *.' This particular conversation was the first talk I had with him. THAT WAS THE REASON MADE ME KEEP MY EYE ON HIM. I made up my mind the old fellow would be pretty fast to sell out. As soon as I see his eye-sight was getting poor I would get around him and feel of him." Record, 133.

In another place he says he watched the business for he saw that his getting it was a mere question of time.

And yet this same waiting, watching, and eager purchaser claimed in his testimony on page 127 testified as follows:

"Question. What importance, if any, did you attach to the statements and representations which were found in those papers of his?"

"Answer. Everything: if it had not been for what he said from time to time in the paper, I should never have dreamed of investing that amount of money. * * * Should not have thought of touching it, and I don't think any other man in the county would touch it as it was." Record, 127. See also the testimony of Beal on pages 376, 377, and 378. Also bottom of page 384.

Courts of equity will not enforce specifically a hard or oppressive agreement, though it relate to a subject matter on which they look with more favor than they do on contracts in restraint of occupation.

In such cases without holding the contract void they frequently leave the party to his remedy at law.

But in this case is not the covenant void even at law for want of consideration? In Hitchcock vs. Coker, 6 Ad. & Ellis, 438, (same case 33d Eng. C. L., 241, 250,) in which for the first time it was laid down that it was not necessary that the consideration received should be proportionate to the value of what the party gives up or loses by the restraint, it was said by Chief Justice Tindal: " If there is no consideration, or a consideration of no real value, the contract in restraint of trade, which in itself is never favored in law, must either be a fraud on the rights of the party restrained, or a mere voluntary contract, a *nudum pactum*, and therefore void."

In Hubbard vs. Miller, 27 Mich., 15, the agreement for restraint was part of the original contract of sale. The mere fact that the property was sold at cost with five per cent. for freight added, did not show that the property was worth the price at the time of sale as understood by the parties; and it could not, therefore, properly be said in that case, that the purchaser paid nothing for the agreed restraint. In this case, however, as clearly appears from the testimony, there was in fact, nothing whatever paid for this covenant. The price had been agreed upon and settled, the deeds made, mortgages assigned, and the bill of sale

Exhibit No. 2, in evidence (being Exhibit B, annexed to the answers,) was about half drawn, before anything was said about any covenant on the part of Chase restraining himself in any way whatever from his occupation. Record.

VII.

The mere sale of the good will of the business without a covenant does not deprive a seller of the right to carry on the same business at the next door.

Sharkle vs. Baker, 14 Vesey, 468.
Cruttwell vs. Sye, 17 Vesey, 334.
6 Ind., 203.
Snowden vs. Noah, Hopkins' Ch. Rep., 347, 351.
Bell vs. Locke, 8 Paige, 74.

VIII.

But assuming the contract to be valid as against Chase, there is no case made against the defendant company. There is no pretense of any contract or obligation in any form, on the part of the corporation, as such, to the complainant. It is not even charged in the bill that the corporation as such had any notice of the restraining covenant between Chase and Beal. The allegation is that the stockholders had knowledge that Beal had made the purchase and was carrying on the business under the name of "Dr. Chase's Steam Printing House," and that Chase had entered into a contract with complainant in reference to the same, and had no right to carry on said business at ANN ARBOR, directly or indirectly. (See bottom of page 6 of Record). The proof shows that in fact, Mr. Krause, one of the corporators, had no knowledge or information of any restraining covenant on the part of Chase, and therefore the allegation of the bill above mentioned is not true. Besides the corporation is a person in law, entirely distinct from all the individual corporators, and the contract of each or all of the corporators in their individual capacity would not bind the corporation, or render it liable to be drawn into litigation as a party. This is elementary law. In Van Allen vs. The Assessors, 3 Wallace, 573, 584, the Supreme Court of the United States said: "The tax on the shares (of a bank) is not a tax on the capital of the bank. The corporation is the owner of all the property of the bank, real and personal, and within the powers confered upon it by the charter, can deal with the corporate property as absolutely as a private individual can deal with his own. This is familiar law, and will be found in every work on the subject of corporations. A striking exemplification may be seen in the case of the Queen vs. Arnoud, 9 Ad. & Ellis, n. s. 806." And the Court further held that the interest of the shareholders in a bank was an entirely distinct and independent interest from the interest or property of the corporation itself. The Queen vs. Arnoud, above referred to, was an application for a mandamus to compel the collector and comptroller of customs of Liverpool to register a ship belonging to the Pacific Steam Navigation Company, a British corporation. Registration had been refused upon the ground that various foreigners residing abroad were stockholders in the corporation, and had an interest in the vessel, and were entitled to share in the profits of its business. By the law of England, foreigners were excluded from the privileges of British ship owners. By the statute, in order to obtain registration it was necessary to make oath "that no foreigner, directly or indirectly, hath any share, or part, or interest," in the vessel. Another statute confined the registration to such ships as "shall wholly belong and continue to wholly belong to her majesty's subjects," and prohibited any person who had taken the oath of allegiance to any foreign state, or who usually resided out of the Queen's dominions from being "the owner in whole or in part directly or indirectly" of a vessel requiring registration.

The Court of Queen's Bench in granting a peremptory mandamus, (Chief Justice Denman delivering the opinion) said: "Now, it appears to us, that the British corporation is. as such, the SOLE OWNER of the ship, and a British subject within the meaning of the fifth section, as far as such a term can be applicable to a corporation, notwithstanding some foreigners may individually have shares in the company, and that such individual members of the corporation, are not entitled, in whole, or in part, directly or indirectly, to be OWNERS of the vessel. The individual members of the corporation, no doubt, are interested, in one sense, in the property of the corporation, as they may derive individual benefit from its increase, or loss from its destruction; but in no LEGAL SENSE are the individual members the owners. If all the individuals of the corporation were duly qualified British subjects, they could not register the vessel in their individual names AS OWNERS, but must register it as belonging wholly to the corporation as owner. * * * "It was contended that the effect might be to defeat the object and policy of the navigation laws in this respect. The individual members of the British corporation might, either originally or by transfer, be all foreigners. Such does not appear to be contemplated or provided for by the act in question. If it be *casus omissus*, and evil consequences arise, they may be remedied by the interference of the legislature, and possibly, though I do not wish to be understood as giving any opinion on this point, by repealing the letters patent as improvidently giving powers operating to defeat the law and public policy; and in future patents, providing against the objection: but, as the case stands, it seems to us that the British corporation is to all intents, the legal owner of the vessel, and entitled to the registry, and that we cannot notice any disqualification of an individual member which might disable him, if owner, from registering the vessel in his own name."

The Supreme Court of Illinois, in the recent case of Porter vs. The Rockford, Rock Island, and St. Louis Railroad Company, decided June, 1874, said: "The legal property of the stockholders is quite distinct from that of the corporation, although the shares of stock have no value, save that which they derive from the corporate property and franchise; and a tax levied on the property of one is not, in a legal sense, levied on the property of the other." The Court in the same case, quoted as part of its opinion, from 2d Redfield on Railways, page 460, sec. 2, 3d ed., as follows: "The interest or right of a shareholder in a corporation is well defined by Shaw, C. J.: 'the right is, strictly speaking, a right to participate in a certain proportion, in the immunities and benefits of the corporation.' This is a right of property, as distinct from the capital stock of a company, as a debt is distinct from a debtor, or the mortgage debt from the mortgaged premises." See Chicago Times, June 22, 1874, for full opinion of Supreme Court of Illinois.

In Second Congregational Society vs. Howard, 16 Pick., 210, 211; Chief Justice Shaw said: "The well-known rule in regard to a corporation, as being a person in law, having rights distinct from those of all its members," settled the question in that case.

In Angell and Ames on Corporations, page 38, note 2, 4th ed., it is said: "One of the greatest distinctions in contemplation of law, between partnership and corporate companies, is that, in the first, the law looks to the individuals of whom the partnership is composed, and knows the partnership no otherwise than as being such number of individuals; while in the second, it sees only the creature of the charter, the body corporate, and knows not the individuals." See also, for distinction between partnerships and corporations, sections 41 and 591, of same book.

It is settled by a series of decisions in the United States Courts that a corporation is a citizen of the State under whose laws it was created, and that the residence of the corporators is of no importance in determining the citizenship of the corporation, under the Judiciary Act, allowing suits between citizens of different States. Ohio and Miss. Railroad Co. vs. Wheeler, 1 Black, 286; 20 Howard, 232; 16 Howard, 314; 2 Howard, 497.

The Court below had less ground for breaking up the business of this corporation by injunctions than the deputy sheriff in Nichols vs. Thomas, 4 Mass., 232, 233, had for arresting one of the "proprietors" (or corporators) of "The President, Directors, and Company of the Union Turnpike Corporation," under an execution commanding him to levy on the goods, etc., "of the said President, Directors, and Company of the Union Turnpike Corporation, and for want thereof to take the bodies of said President, Directors, and Company."

This corporation did not obtain its right to print and publish from either Chase or Beal, and is in no way affected by any personal rights or liabilities of those persons as between themselves. It is rather difficult to see how any NOTICE to the corporation, if one had been alleged and proved, could affect its rights. But, as before stated, there is no such allegation or proof as to the corporation. There is no proof whatever in the case impeaching the genuineness of the corporation, or throwing any doubt on the validity of the stock of Messrs. Watson, Deans, Krause, and

King therein, or on the fact of the absolute sale by Chase to the other stockholders of his entire stock.

If, as the court below seemed to think, there was no distinction between a corporation and the corporators, upon what rule of justice could the stock of Henry Krause be destroyed by injunction, since his investment was made without being under any obligation to Beal, and without any notice in fact on his part of any restraining covenant on the part of Chase?

IX.

There is nothing in the contract between Chase and Beal whereby Chase is restrained from the writing of any book. The sale of "Dr. Chase's Recipes, (being his first book,) and the other things mentioned in the contract did not affect or impair the rights of Chase as an author, except to transfer his interests under the copyrights sold. (See the discussion of this subject on pages 40 and 41, in the brief of Lawrence & Sawyer.) The defendant company having the general right to print and publish had as full a right to print and publish a book written by Chase as any other. Whether the new book is a better or more popular book than the one sold to Beal, or whether its sale will tend to supercede the sale of the former book is entirely immaterial, since its publication and sale is a mere exercise of a right of the company. In the absence of a valid restraining covenant, Chase himself was authorized, not only to write, but also to publish as many books as he pleased on the same subject, and of the same general character as the one sold to Beal, so long as he did not induce the public to believe the book to be the same IDENTICAL book as the former one, and so long as he was guilty of no infringement of copyright.

 Hogg vs. Kirby, 8 Vesey, 215.
 Snowden vs. Noah. Hopkins, Ch. 347.
 Bell vs. Locke, 8 Paige, 75.
 Crutwell vs. Lye, 17 Vesey, 341.
 See also opinion of Judge Higby in the former suit between these parties, Record, 504 to 507.

The " Second Receipt Book," published by the defendant corporation is carefully distinguished by its title page from "Dr. Chase's Recipe Book" which he sold to Beal, and its volume, contents, and appearance are so different that there is no possibility of one book being mistaken for the other. No infringement of copyright is pretended, and if there were, no remedy therefor could be sought in a State court.

Palmer vs DeWitt, 47 N. Y., 536.
Wheaton vs Peters, 8 Peters, 668.
Dudley vs. Mayhew, 3 Comstock, 14.

X.

The decree is broader than the contract. After restraining Chase from being directly or indirectly engaged in the business of printing or publishing in the State of Michigan, so long as Beal remains in that business at Ann Arbor, it restrains him from printing or publishing, or being in any manner, directly or indirectly, engaged OR INTERESTED in printing or publishing in this State, "Dr. Chase's Family Physician, Farrier, Bee-Keeper and Second Receipt Book," so long as Beal shall continue his printing business at Ann Arbor, and shall continue to print and publish "Dr. Chase's Recipes, or Information for Everybody." As it is not probable that mere tautology was intended by the insertion of the words "OR INTERESTED," the intention must have been to impose a restraint beyond the "engaging, directly or indirectly, in the business of printing and publishing." The purpose of complainant's counsel in so drafting the decree undoubtedly was to deprive Chase of his author's royalty, and to embarrass the company in the performance of its contract to pay Chase for his interest in the copyright—which results are not within the words of Chase's contract. And the injunction decree restraining the company from carrying on the printing or publishing business in connection with Chase, or wherein Chase shall be directly or indirectly engaged OR INTERESTED, and from printing or publishing in connection as partners or otherwise with Chase, OR FOR HIS BENEFIT in whole or in part, &c., "Dr. Chase's Family Physician," &c., is justly subject to the same criticism.

The decree goes the vindictive length of depriving Chase of a right to INCOME from a book which he was at liberty to write, though he shall not be engaged in any way in the business of printing or publishing it. It is not content with excluding him from his occupation of printer and publisher, but it refuses him the rights of authorship which the covenant left intact.

I also call attention to the fact clearly established by the proofs, that soon after Beal's purchase, he changed the name of the printing establishment from " Dr. Chase's Steam Printing House" to " Courier Steam Printing House, R. A. Beal, Proprietor," and continued such change of name in the business of the establishment and in its imprint, until since the filing of the bill in this case.

XI.

The defendants had a right to set up in their answers, facts which occurred prior to their being put in.

Lyon vs. Brooks, 2 Edwards Ch. 110.

Upon any view of the case the decree should be reversed as to both defendants, and the bill dismissed. The part of the bill wherein the complainant seeks to secure to himself all Chase's letters, is, if possible, more indefensible than the decree appealed from; but the discussion of that subject, as well as the question of damages, arising under the second decree, will be reserved for a separate brief, unless the court shall think proper to order that both appeals shall be heard together at the present time.

HIRAM J. BEAKES,
Of Counsel for Defendants.

FULL OPINION

OF

JUDGE CHRISTIANCY

IN THE CASE OF

R. A. Beal vs. Alvan W. Chase and the Ann Arbor Printing and Publishing Company.

RENDERED FEBURARY 26, 1875,
IN THE PRESENCE OF A FULL BENCH, ALL THE JUDGES CONCURRING ON ALL THE ESSENTIAL POINTS.

ANN ARBOR, MICH.:
COURIER STEAM PRINTING HOUSE.
1875

JUDGE CHRISTIANCY'S OPINION.

The bill in this case was filed July 14th, 1873, in the Washtenaw Circuit, for the purpose of enjoining the defendants from carrying on, or being directly or indirectly engaged in the business of printing or publishing in the State of Michigan, so long as complainant should be engaged in that business at Ann Arbor, and from taking and receiving from the postoffice at Ann Arbor any letters addressed to said Chase, which should not have upon them a designation of the number of his private letter box, or from interfering with their delivery to complainant; and from publishing or making sale, either directly or indirectly, of a book written by said Chase, known as "The New Book—Dr. Chase's Family Physician, Farrier, Bee-keeper, and Second Receipt Book." As an abstract of the bill and answers will accompany the report, it is unnecessary here to notice their several features or allegations, further than to say, that the bill is appropriate to the state of facts shown by the evidence, so far as such facts warrant the relief asked.

Nor shall we enter into a discussion or analysis of the large volume of evidence in the record and the particular reasons which have led us where the evidence is conflicting, to the conclusions at which we have arrived; but we shall proceed to state the main facts and essential features upon which, in our view, the decision of the case must depend, as we find them established by the evidence.

Some fourteen years prior to the sale by Chase to Beal, presently to be mentioned, Chase had published a book, under the title of "Dr. Chase's Recipes; or, Information for Everybody," which proved to be very popular, and the demand for which was very great.

For the first seven years after its first publication, the sale of this book had been made principally by Dr. Chase himself traveling about the country for that purpose. But the sales becoming so large, and the profits so considerable, and the public demand still increasing, he had, several years prior to the sale to Beal, established in Ann Arbor a printing-house and bindery, in which the printing and binding of this book was carried on, and in connection with which he published a newspaper called "THE PENINSULAR COURIER AND FAMILY VISITANT," and carried on the business of job-printing and binding. The establishment being known as "Dr. Chase's Steam Printing-House," and as "The Courier Steam Printing-House." This business and the establishment in which it was carried on—at first comparatively small, had rapidly increased and grown larger in course of time, and by adding from time to time, more presses, type, tools, and apparatus, and enlarging the building in which it was carried on, the whole had become one of the best and most complete establishments in the Northwest, for the business of printing and book-binding, and beyond the printing and binding of Dr. Chase's books, enjoyed a large and increasing patronage, soliciting work from all parts of the State as well as from abroad, and actually obtaining work from various parts, and a large portion of the State, (though as yet none from the Upper Peninsula), and a considerable amount from other States. In the meantime the mode of selling his book had been changed. He no longer traveled himself for that purpose; but the books were furnished to persons in various parts of the country and in the various States, who chose to undertake the sale as traveling agents, or rather traveling booksellers, who paid the money for the books at a wholesale price, before the books were taken or sent from the office, and mostly sent out to those persons upon orders sent by letter by them to Dr. Chase, accompanied with the money, or a draft, or post-office order. Letters of this kind had become very numerous, and the sales unprecedentedly large, over 325,000 in all having been sold up to the close of the year 1868, and about 375,000 when the sale was made to Beal; and as stated over his own signature from time to time in his paper, to which he referred Beal when negotiating for the purchase, the total receipts of the office and business, including sales of the book, were for the year 1866, about of $55,000, of which $47,254.34 was for the book alone; for the year 1867, total receipts were $66,034.68, of which $57,781.36 was for the book; and for the year 1868, the sales of the book amounted to about $11,000 less; but the other business of the establishment had so increased that the profits for the year were about the same. Letters in reference to the book, many of which contained money, drafts, or postoffice orders, often amounted to from 100 to 150 per week, and brought in from $300 to $400 up to over $1,200 per week, much the larger portion of which was clear profit. The sale of the book was the great source of profit, and this book, together with his newspaper, and the prompt and excellent manner in which the job-work of the office was done, had made Dr. Chase well known to, and popular with the public, and had given him and his establishment a high reputation which attracted a large amount of business; so that as he represented in his paper to which Beal during the negotiation was referred for the facts, he was receiving orders from every section of the State, from Wisconsin and from Indiana, and all over the Western States; still as appears by the evidence, much the larger portion of the business was furnished from different parts of this State; and from considerable portions of which, and especially the whole Upper Peninsula no orders had yet been received. The book was the main support, however, of the office, and as he more than once intimated in his paper, but for that he could not have made the other branches of business very profitable at the prices for which his work was done. And for the last year the sale of the book had materially diminished, the country, (with the exception of the Southern States) having been pretty well canvassed; and the book had recently been offered to the trade (the regular booksellers) in many of the States, the sale by traveling agents being still continued as before.

Such substantially was the condition of the business when, on the 30th of August, 1869, Chase sold out to Beal the printing and binding establishment and the business connected with it, the book (and two other books mentioned in the contract of sale), and the newspaper and its subscription list, as well as the lot and building where the business was carried on, the entire apparatus for printing and binding, and the good will of the business. Some two years previous to this, however, some negotiations had been commenced between them in reference to a sale, an offer had been made by Chase to Beal, to sell for about $37,000, which Beal, after some days reflection, concluded not to accept. But he still continued to watch the progress of the business with the view of making the purchase at some future time, believing it, as he expressed it, the best thing in Ann Arbor. And Chase, though he had greatly enlarged his office and increased his business, had in the meantime become anxious to sell.

Some days prior to the sale, the parties met at Ann Arbor, and entered upon negotiations. Chase made representations of the nature and extent of the property and business, the success of the book, the profits of the book and business, which he represented to be large, and the business in a flourishing condition, extending generally over the State, and into adjoining States, as already noticed, and constantly increasing; and explaining the mode in which it was carried on and the book sold; which representations, Beal alleges in his bill, and testifies, were generally and in the main true. He enlarged upon the popularity the book had attained, its great usefulness, and the reputation he had acquired and his establishment; and that this would be of great advantage to Beal should he make the purchase, and said that it would be likely to command the market for many years; and that no other book would be likely to come into competition with or supersede it. As a reason for wishing to sell out he stated that he was getting advanced in years; his sight was getting poor, and his health failing; that he had now enough to live on, and wished to retire from so arduous and extensive a business; and if he continued to do any business, should wish to get into a business more easily managed, and which would not require so much constant care and attention, and would be more manageable for a family like his; that if Beal should purchase him out, he would aid him in getting acquainted with and starting the business, and would, as Beal testifies, devote six months, but as Chase testifies, three months, to this end; spoke of the great amount of the letters and orders for the book, and for work to be done, which were continually being received, enclosing money, drafts, or postoffice orders, which would go into Beal's hands, and would continue to come for the book for years to come.

Finally on Saturday the 28th of August, 1869, the price and terms of payment were verbally agreed upon; the price was nominally sixty-five thousand dollars, of which thirty-five thousand was to be paid down in cash, and securities received as cash, and for the balance thirty thousand dollars, Chase was to receive certain lands in Minnesota and certain real estate at Sauk Rapids, Minnesota, with a hotel upon it, and certain furniture and personal property; all of which Chase took at his own risk, as to value, having made such inquiries concerning it as he chose to make. And on Monday, the 30th of August, the parties went to the office of Mr. Gott, in Ann Arbor, to have the papers drawn and the necessary transfers made for carrying out the arrangement. The real estate of Chase in Ann Arbor was conveyed to Beal by a deed of Chase and wife, for the consideration (specified) of twenty-five thousand dollars; the proper conveyance made by Beal to Chase of the Minnesota property. The contract or instrument transferring the printing, publishing and binding, the newspaper, the book, etc., and the business connected with it, seems to have been the last instrument drawn, the details of which do not appear to have been in all respects previously specified and agreed upon. When this was partly drawn Beal said that "of course Chase was not to go into business again;" Chase replied that, "nothing has been said on that point"—to which Beal said, "of course, you are not; and it must be embodied in this paper." Chase then told Gott to insert, that while Beal should remain in the printing and publishing business in Ann Arbor, he, Chase, should not engage in it in Ann Arbor. But Beal not being satisfied with this, it was finally agreed that this restraining clause should be made co-extensive with the State, as it now stands in the contract. We mention this only because it is now insisted by the defendants' counsel that there was no consideration for this restraining clause, aside from what had already been verbally agreed upon for the purchase, and that, therefore, there was no adequate consideration for this restraint upon Chase. But as there is nothing in the evidence tending to show that Beal would have consummated the purchase for the price given without this stipulation, and it satisfactorily appears that he would not, we see no ground for any question of the adequacy of the consideration, if this provision is in other respects valid. Upon this question of consideration the case falls directly within the principle announced by this Court in the *Hubbard v. Miller, 27 Mich. 15*, and this point need not be further noticed.

The contract or instrument in which this restraining provision occurs, is in these words: "This agreement, made the 30th day of August in the year of our Lord one thousand eight hundred and sixty-nine, between Alvan W. Chase of the city of Ann Arbor, in the county of Washtenaw, in the State of Michigan, and Rice A. Beal of the same place, witnesseth, that the said party of the first part, grants, bargains, sells and conveys, unto the said party of the second part, (in consideration of the sum of forty thousand dollars to him in hand paid) the machinery, boiler, engine, presses, tools, furniture, and stock of whatever name or nature, in the building occupied by said Chase, as his steam printing office, and this day sold by him to the said party of the second part, together with all accounts for unfinished work on which payment has not already been made; together with the subscription list of the PENINSULAR COURIER AND FAMILY VISITANT, and also the copyright of a book called 'Dr. Chase's Recipes, or Information for Everybody,' and also one other book called 'The Judd Family,' also a book called 'Reminiscences of a Voyage Around the World'—a copyright of which is to be hereafter obtained, together with the *good will of the business of printing and publishing, and also the right to use the name of Dr. Chase in connection with said books*, all the stereotypes and electro-plate for said books now completed, and also the book-bindery tools and stocks, and all contracts for printing and publishing, together with all moneys to be hereafter received upon jobs or books unfinished. *And the said party of the first part also agrees that while said Beal remains in said business of printing and publishing in Ann Arbor, he will not either directly or indirectly engage in the business of printing and publishing in the State of Michigan.*

And the said Beal on his part, if he choses, may carry on said business, and he shall have the exclusive right, under the name of 'Dr. Chase's Steam Printing House,' and may add R. A. Beal, proprietor, and he also agrees to fulfill all contracts heretofore entered into by said party of the first part for work, printing and advertising or publishing, and is to receive all moneys unpaid on said contracts. He is also to furnish the COURIER AND VISITANT to all subscribers for the balance of their subscription year, and receive all unpaid subscriptions. All property belonging to workmen, and all books or papers left for binding are excepted out of this sale; but it is intended to include all furniture, tables, desks, and everything used to carry on said business of printing, publishing and book-binding. The party of the second part is also to have the privilege for one year of using the cistern and privy, on lot west of Steam Printing House for engine and hands of the building. Beal is to pay taxes assessed to Dr. Chase on the property this day conveyed to said Beal, real and personal, for the year 1869.

The party of the first part also sells to the party of the second part, his gray horse and establishment purchased by him of Rev. H. S. White, including buggy, cutter and harness, saddle, bridle, buffalo robe, bells, etc.

Said Beal is to have the privilege of receiving the letters connected with said business, and opening the same.

Witness our hands and seals, etc.

Signed by CHASE AND BEAL.

The papers were all executed and delivered on the 30th of August, and on that day or the next, the parties went together to the postoffice, *and Chase then publicly, in the presence of the clerks, told Col. Grant, the postmaster, that he had sold out his business to Beal and everything connected with it, and that Beal was thereafter to have all his correspondence and money orders, etc., directed the postmaster to deliver to him all letters directed to him, Chase, including registered letters, for which Beal, he said, was authorized to receipt in his name, and that he was authorized to sign his name in all matters connected with the office, and the business,* that Beal was to have the postoffice drawer previously used by Chase in connection with his office business; and he directed the postmaster to put all letters that came directed to him, or to the printing and publishing house, into that box for Beal, unless such letters bore on the face of them a direction to his own private box, (which he said he would take,) or the number of his residence, *saying at the same time, that he was no longer Dr. Chase.* This direction to the postmaster was in accordance with the parol understanding had between the parties during the negotiations, in which it was understood that Beal was to receive and open all such correspondence, and whenever he found a letter which pertained to Dr. Chase personally and not to the business, he was to return it to Chase or put it in his private box.

And Chase some time after this had a printed card and letter-head put on his private letters to his correspondents, stating *that all letters intended for himself or family should also have upon them Postoffice Box 351, otherwise they would go to his former printing house and be opened by strangers.*

For about three years this arrangement relative to the correspondence seems to have been scrupulously adhered to, and the letters received, the larger portion of which were in reference to the sale of the book, which was principally sold in this way, amounted to from three or four per day up to thirty per day, a very large portion containing orders for the book, and money drafts or postoffice orders to pay for them. And among the letters thus received, addressed to Chase, not *one in four or five hundred, if indeed one in a thousand, had reference to the private business of Chase,* or any business except that sold to Beal. And though the sale of the book had gradually somewhat declined, as the demand for it was being supplied, it was still very large, and the business of the printing and binding establishment was large, prosperous and profitable.

But in the meantime, Doctor Chase had commenced writing, and was preparing for publication, a new book upon a somewhat similar plan, though containing none of the matter of the first book, and entitled (upon the title page) "Dr. Chase's Family Physician, Farrier, Bee-Keeper, and Second Receipt Book," and being desirous of publishing the same himself, and at Ann Arbor, where he resided, had consulted counsel as to the validity of the restraining clause in his contract with Beal, and had come to the conclusion *that it was not legally binding upon him, and therefore, as he testifies, that he was under no obligation to abide by it.* He still, however, kept the entire consideration which he had received, and did not return or offer to return it, or any part of it.

But he met Beal and proposed to purchase back the property, offering to pay in other property to the amount of some $15,000 to $20,000. Beal, however, asked $75,000, and offered to sell for that. Several interviews were had in reference to it, but resulted in nothing. In one of these interviews Chase intimated for the first time that his contract not to go into the printing and publishing business was not worth the paper it was written on, and that he had a right to go into the business in Ann Arbor, which, however, he said he should not do, as he had given his word. At length, however, in another interview, he told Beal very decidedly that unless he would sell out he should go into business again; that though it would cost some money to start an office, there were men *ready to help him who did not like him (Beal) better than he did.* And Beal having heard of the efforts of Chase to buy another printing establishment, and knowing or believing that there was not room for two such establishments at Ann Arbor without such competition as would render them unprofitable, *became alarmed and anxious to sell. But Chase was no longer inclined to purchase, but said t at if he, Beal, had sold when he wanted him to, it would have been all right, but now he was in a better shape, and would not buy at all.*

Chase thereupon soon after, in the latter part of July, 1872, rented a building, got in presses and printing material, began establishing the printing and publishing business, and had commenced setting type for the new book, when the association or corporation known as "The Ann Arbor Printing and Publishing Company" was formed, the articles of association for which are dated August 26, 1872, filed with the Secretary of State August 28, and with the county clerk of Washtenaw on the 30th of August, 1872. This corporation was located at Ann Arbor. Its objects are declared to be, to do general printing and publishing business, to print, publish, bind and manufacture books, periodicals, newspapers, tracts, documents, and other publications. Its capital was to be $50,000, divided into 500 shares. The stockholders, with the shares taken by each, were declared to be as follows:

Alvan W. Chase,	250 shares.
James C. Watson,	200 "
Henry S. Dean,	15 "
Sedgwick Dean,	15 "
Zina P. King,	10 "
Henry Krause,	10 "

All of whom resided at Ann Arbor, and each was declared to be a director of the Company. A President, Vice-President, Secretary and Treasurer were provided for. One half the capital stock ($25,000) was paid in, Chase putting in the stock, and material of the printing house he had just commenced, as a part of payment; and this was merged in the new Company. *Some of the stockholders had long been aware of the contract between Chase and Beal, and of the nature of the restraining clause in it, and all the others, with the possible (though to our mind not probable) exception of Krause, had notice of it before the corporation was fully completed or went into business, but concluded to take the risk of its invalidity.*

Dr. Chase, who owned one-half the stock, was made *president and superintendent* of the Company, and so remained when the bill in this case was filed. He was the only stockholder who had ever before been engaged in or carried on the printing or publishing business, though one other stockholder, Watson, had, when a boy learned to set type, and he had been the author of some books, and contemplated the writing and publishing of others. The Company also established and published a weekly newspaper, the "Ann Arbor Register," and entered upon the general printing and publishing business. Their establishment in a short time, by the addition of presses, type, and apparatus for the various branches of the work, rivaling that of Beal, though not equal in extent or capacity.

Dr. Chase being still engaged in preparing his new book, which had been previously advertised to be completed by the 1st of December, 1872, but which was not yet completed, on the 3d day of April, 1873, entered into a formal written contract with the Company, by which he purports to give to the Company the exclusive right to publish this new book, during the term of its copyright; the Company to publish the work in good style as soon as possible after receiving the manuscript, and at all times to keep a supply of it for sale, and use all reasonable efforts to advance its sale, and paying to him *ten cents on each dollar* of the retail price of all the books sold; and the new book was issued April 23d, 1873.

It is proper to say here that from the evidence and all the circumstances of the case, Chase himself was the first to suggest and instigate the formation of this company, and was anxious for and active in promoting its formation, though Watson was the most active member in actually effecting it. *We are also entirely satisfied that the publication and sale of Dr. Chase's New Book, the Second Receipt Book, which from the unprecedented sales of and great profits of his first book, it was believed would prove equally profitable, constituted the main inducement for the formation of the Printing and Publishing Company,* and that the stockholders believed the sale of this book would form the greatest and most reliable source of profit to this company, as the first book had to Dr. Chase's Printing House (since sold to Beal), and that, without this new book and the prospects of profit to be derived from it, this printing company would not have been formed.

But to return to the correspondence, the company having been formed and about commencing, if it had not already commenced the business of *printing and publishing under his superintendence, Chase on the 19th day of September, 1872, countermanded his previous direction to the postmaster, by the following letter:*

ANN ARBOR, Mich.,
September 19, 1872.

POSTMASTER, ANN ARBOR, MICH.—

Sir: You will hereafter place all letters addressed to me in my box, unless there is something in the address of the letter to indicate that it is intended for the publisher of Dr. Chase's Recipes or the proprietor of Dr. Chase's Steam Printing House.

[Signed]   A. W. CHASE.

The first notice Beal had of this was that from that time he began to receive letters in reference to the book and business of the office (addressed as they all along had been to Dr. Chase) which had been opened by Chase, and on which he had written Beal's name and put them in the office. These letters mainly related to the first receipt book, as formerly, asking for the book, seeking agencies, and many of them containing remittances of money, drafts, or postoffice orders. But *from about this time the number of letters, the amount of remittances coming to Beal's hands and the sale of the book began perceptibly to decline beyond any previous rate, and more and more rapidly as the time passed on, a principal reason for which will appear as we proceed to have been the use made by Chase of the correspondence belonging to Beal, the circulars issued and efforts made by Chase for the sale of the new or "Second Receipt Book." In April or May, 1873, Chase ceased to hand over to Beal even the letters containing orders and remittances for the old book, but retained them,* sending the old book, however, when the order was express, but *sending also to these persons and to those agents who were engaged in selling the old book for Beal, circulars describing and extolling the "New Receipt Book"* inviting them to undertake its sale as a more saleable and a better and more complete book, and likely to supersede the first receipt book. As a specimen, I hear quote what Dr. Chase says in one of the printed circulars sent out by him, (purporting to be superintendent of the printing company) to the agents or persons known by him to be engaged *in the sale of the old book for Beal (and opening as he did all the letters coming in his name pertaining to Beal's business correspondence and agencies, he had every facility for ascertaining the list of them)* he says (after enumerating the various contents of the new book) *"and as no bookstore man will buy even an old edition of a book after a new one is got out, then will not this rule hold good with an entire new book by the same author, which not only covers the ground of the old, but is fully four times as extensive, and contains entirely new matter, as compared with the first. Even those who have the old ought to have the new."* The circulars were headed "Dr. Chase's New Receipt Book."

CIRCULAR TO AGENTS.

The letters in which these circulars were sent out to those who had sent for the first or old book, and those engaged in the sale of it were headed in print—

"A. W. Chase, President and Superintendent.
J. C. Watson, Vice-President.
Zina P. King, Secretary.
Henry S. Dean, Treasurer.
Organized August, 1872.

The Ann Arbor Printing and Publishing Company, publishers of Dr. Chase's Family Physician, Farrier, Bee-Keeper and Second Receipt Book, issued April 23. Retail price, $2.00."

And as another specimen, and it is a specimen of the kind of efforts made to make the new book supplant the old, and to interfere with the proper business of Beal connected with the book sold to him, the following is a letter under the above letter-head:

"ANN ARBOR, June 3d, 1873.

MR. J. D. BRACE.—

Sir: Your favor of the 1st is at hand. I sold out the old book nearly four years ago, and have in the last three years got out a second entirely new book, and as no book-store men want to buy an old book after a new one is out, you may feel the same way, at least the people here do. The enclosed circular gives prices and a descriptive circular, and "Register," our newspaper, will give you an idea of the new book and its sale. We will wait your further orders, remarking, however, that we confine our men to one county only, and one county for each assistant. We sell in no other way. Respectfully,   A. W. CHASE,
Superintendent.

Other similar letters were sent to parties who had enclosed a remittance for the old book, which was also sent.

This correspondence having relation to the book and business sold to Beal, though continued in the name of Dr. Chase, as it was understood and agreed it might be, it cannot be denied, was just as much the property and correspondence of Beal's as if it had been carried on by Beal in his own name; and Dr. Chase had no more right to control it, or to avail himself of any benefit to arise from or information contained in it. And as by an express provision of the written contract, the validity of which is not disputed, Beal, and not Chase, was to have the right not only of "receiving" but of "opening" the correspondence, we cannot doubt that if the position of the parties and the case had been reversed, and Beal had taken, and opened, and made use of, in the same way, correspondence belonging to Chase and pertaining to his business, Dr. Chase would readily have seen and felt the unfairness and injustice of such a course of conduct. But it will suffice to say here that the natural and direct, if not also the necessary effect of this course of conduct in reference to the correspondence, as well as in getting up and establishing, and aiding to carry on a rival establishment for printing, publishing, binding, etc., was to lessen the sale of the receipt book which had been sold to Beal, and to diminish his business in all its departments as well as its profits. And there is no room for doubt that Chase's conduct in reference to the correspondence and the use he made of it, were purposely intended to have this effect, as respected the success and sale of the first book. The evidence tends to show the extent of the loss and injury thus caused.

And though the amount is not susceptible of accurate calculation, and can only be matter of probable estimate, the question being affected by so many considerations and the actual falling off in the receipts being in some small degree attributable to other causes. Yet, upon a careful consideration of the testimony, and making due allowance for other causes of diminution of receipts, I think the loss or damage fairly traceable to the unwarrantable interference with the correspondence belonging to Beal, the still more unwarrantable use made of the information thereby obtained, and to the rivalry created and the amount of business and profits diverted from Beal, by the establishment of the printing and publishing company cannot safely be placed below (if it is not in fact above) the sum found by the Court below and fixed by the decree; and I see no reason for disturbing the amount thus fixed, if damages be allowable at all.

To proceed with the history of the case; Chase had on the 19th of September, 1872, countermanded his directions to the postmaster, and taken possession of the correspondence as already stated.

Beal, on the 17th day of October, 1872, filed his bill in the Circuit Court for the County of Washtenaw, in Chancery, against Chase and the Ann Arbor Printing and Publishing Company, the principal object and only express prayer (for relief) of which, was to restrain the defendants from printing and publishing the Second or New Receipt Book, on the ground that the title of the book, was an infringement upon the proprietory right of complainant to the copyright of the first book sold to him, and calculated and intended to lead the public to believe, that the book about to be published, was but a new, enlarged, and more complete edition of said first book. The bill, however, sets forth briefly, and with much less particularity than in the present bill, much of the same matter found in the latter. The sale by Chase to Beal of the first book and the printing house and business, the undertaking of Chase not to go into the printing and publishing business in the State, the agreement in reference to the correspondence, that Chase had "recently entered upon a plan to disregard and violate his said agreement in relation to said sale and purchase," complainant's continuance in the business of printing and publishing, the organization of the printing company, which is charged to be a sham got up by Chase to evade the terms of his agreement, &c. The advertisements issued in relation to the forthcoming Second Receipt Book, and the injury likely to result to complainant from this course of conduct; and praying besides the specific relief asked "such other and further relief as may be agreeable to equity and good conscience."

In pursuance of a previous order to that effect, the hearing of an application for a preliminary injunction on this bill, was had on the 22d of October, and the motion was finally, on the 25th of October, denied by the Circuit Judge.

On the 4th of December, 1872, the defendant Chase and the Printing Company, filed their separate answers, going over much of the same ground as their answers to the present bill. The case remained in this condition until the 14th day of July, 1873, when it was discontinued by the complainant and the present bill was thereupon filed on the same day, and a preliminary injunction having been granted as prayed by the bill, two successive motions to dissolve the injunction were made by defendants upon affidavits and heard by the Judge prior to the filing of an answer by either of them, both of which were denied.

The Printing Company filed its answer to the present bill August 5th, and defendant Chase August 11th, 1873.

In the meantime, Chase had, on the first day of August, (18 days after the filing of the bill) executed an instrument of that date, purporting in consideration of $12,500 to sell, assign and convey to the other members or stockholders of the Ann Arbor Printing and Publishing Company (in certain specified proportions to each) all his stock and all his rights as a stockholder, and his subscriptions for stock in said company, he to be kept harmless from any subsequent assessments on the stock which they agreed to do; and on the same day resigned the office of President and Superintendent of the Company, which the remaining Board of Directors accepted, he still, however, retaining his interest in the contract made with the Company for publishing the new book.

This transfer (which Chase swears was made for the purpose of getting the book published by the Company) is set up in the answers as a ground for denying the relief prayed by the bill; and two successive motions were made— the first by the Company for a dissolution of the injunction after its answer was filed and before that of Chase was filed, which was denied. The other, by both defendants, after the filing of Chase's answer, for the modification of the injunction, which was so far granted on the 4th of September as to permit Chase to take from the postoffice all letters addressed to him, unless there was something in the address of the letter to indicate that it was intended for the publisher of Dr. Chase's Recipes, or the proprietor of Dr. Chase's Steam Printing House. But the injunction was continued against all the defendants in all other respects, as prayed for by the bill. This the defendants seem to have found somewhat embarrassing, and all the remaining stockholders of the Ann Arbor Printing and Publishing Company, with one Franklin M. Chase, a nephew of Dr. Chase, organized a stock company at Toledo, Ohio, under the style of "The Chase Publishing Company of Toledo, Ohio," with a capital of $10,000. Franklin M. Chase, who was the book-keeper of the Ann Arbor Company, being the secretary of this. This Company was obviously and essentially the same, and under the same control, as the Ann Arbor Company, established for the sole and only purpose of publishing Dr. Chase's new book, which the Ann Arbor Company had been restrained from publishing in this State, and doing no other business. And on the 30th day of September, 1873, the "Ann Arbor Printing and Publishing Company," by an instrument of that date, purports to convey to the "Chase Publishing Company" all the right of the former Company in and to the agreement between it and Chase for the printing of the new or Second Receipt Book; and upon this instrument Chase, on the 18th of November following, endorsed his assent to this transfer, and to the substitution of the obligations of the one Company for those of the other, he holding himself under the like obligations to the new as he had been to the old Company; and the publication of the book has since been carried on at Toledo.

The case having been heard upon the pleadings and upon the proofs taken in open court, and submitted, the Court, on the first day of June, 1874, rendered a decree disposing of a part of the cause, but reserving certain questions in the cause for further consideration. This decree, so far as rendered on the first day of June, was substantially that, 1st. Chase be absolutely enjoined and restrained from carrying on, or being directly or indirectly engaged in the business of printing or publishing in the State of Michigan, so long as Beal shall remain in or continue to carry on the business of printing and publishing in the city of Ann

Arbor; (and more especially) from printing or publishing, or being directly or indirectly engaged or interested in printing or publishing, *in this State*, the Second Receipt Book (specifying fully its title), so long as complainant shall continue to carry on the printing and publishing business in the city of Ann Arbor, and to print and publish the First Receipt Book—mentioned in the contract—but we do not understand this portion of the decree as aimed at or intended to affect any right of Chase as an author of the Second Receipt Book or any other book; but merely to restrain him from the business of printing and publishing the book in this State.

2d. The decree restrains the Ann Arbor Printing and Publishing Company from carrying on or continuing the business of printing or publishing in this State, *in connection with the defendant Chase*, or wherein said Chase shall be directly or indirectly engaged or interested, and (more especially) from printing or publishing *in connection* as partners or otherwise *with said Chase*, or for his benefit in whole or in part, within the State, the Second Receipt Book, so long as complainant shall remain in the business of printing and publishing in Ann Arbor, and shall continue to print and publish the First Receipt Book. But this decree would allow either Chase or the Printing and Publishing Company to go into the business of printing and publishing the Second Receipt Book, whenever Beal should cease and give up the business of printing and publishing the First Receipt Book at Ann Arbor; and the decree is thus far less extensive than the restraining clause in the contract.

After thus disposing of so much of the case as depended upon the validity of the restraining clause of Chase's contract, this first decree proceeds as follows:

"It is further in like manner ordered, adjudged and decreed, that as to the letters in relation to said business in said contract in said bill mentioned, the injunction heretofore granted and issued in this case be and the same is hereby retained and held in full force and virtue as modified by this Court on the 4th day of September, 1873, until the further order of this Court, and that the question of damages and costs to be recovered by said complainant in this cause, as well as the changing or modifying of the said injunction in regard to the receiving of the letters aforesaid, and all questions involved in this case, not finally disposed of by this decree, be and the same are hereby reserved for the further consideration of this Court."

From this decree the defendants Chase and the Printing and Publishing Company separately appealed to this Court on the 24th day of June, 1874. The return of this appeal, with all the pleadings and proofs, being filed in this Court in July following. This first appeal was argued in this Court in October last. But in the meantime the Circuit Court, on the 16th September, 1874, proceeded by a further decree to dispose of the other questions in the case, the further consideration of which had been reserved on the first of June.

This latter decree is in substance, that Chase and the Printing and Publishing Company, their counsellors, attorneys, etc., do absolutely desist and refrain from taking or receiving from the postoffice in Ann Arbor any letter or letters received or that may be received at said office, addressed to said Chase, which shall not have upon them a designation of the number of said Chase's private letter-box at said office, or in any manner interfering to prevent the delivery of the same to complainant, and from appropriating to his or their use any such letters, or any information therein contained, or any money drafts or postoffice money orders, transmitted in or with any such letters, so long as complainant shall continue in the business of printing and publishing in said city of Ann Arbor. And further, that said Chase and said Company do pay to complainant, and that complainant recover of them, the sum of $10,-316.36, for the damages sustained by complainant after the making of the contract with Beal, and prior to the commencement of this suit, in consequence of the carrying on by the defendants of the printing and publishing business in the city of Ann Arbor, and the interfering with and withholding the letters and correspondence pertaining to said business, in violation of the rights of complainant, as stipulated in the contract between Chase and Beal, and that complainant recover his costs to be taxed—that execution issue, etc.

This last decree was also appealed from, and was argued in this Court at the January term—so that both appeals are now before us for disposition,

It is objected by the defendants that the second decree, or that disposing of the questions reserved upon making the first, is void, being made after the cause upon the first appeal was pending in this Court; and reference is made to *Section 5181, Comp. L. 1871*, which provides that upon the entering of such appeal "all further proceedings in the cause in the Circuit Court in chancery shall be stayed until otherwise ordered by the Supreme Court." But notwithstanding this statute, we have frequently entertained appeals from decrees which disposed only of a part or some particular branch of a cause; and any decree or order may be appealed from, which disposes of the rights of a party upon any independent branch of a case, even though the case, in some other of its phases, may not yet be ripe for a hearing. And we have never held, nor do I think it has been the understanding of the profession, that this statute prohibited any further proceedings in the court below upon a separate and independent branch of the case which could in no way affect the branch of the case covered by the appeal. Again, if the "further proceedings" prohibited by the statute were understood to include any other proceedings than such as might otherwise be taken by or at the instance of the parties—which I think may be questionable—still I can hardly think it was intended to prohibit a judge, who had heard a whole case, and had decided, and made a decree upon a single branch of it, from taking further time to consider and dispose of other branches of it, in no way affecting the first. The object of the statute, I think, was that this same question or subject matter should not be subject to litigation in both courts at the same time. It was not the fault of the appellee that the Court did not decide the whole case at once and make a decree upon all its branches at the same time, and he ought not to be made to suffer from this action of the Court. And it would be the height of injustice to him to hold that he had lost the whole benefit of his bill, and of the litigation upon all branches of the cause not covered by the first decree, because the judge, without any agency of his, had chosen to decide a part of it on one day and a part upon another.

At most, therefore, in my view, I think this action of the Court should be treated as a mere irregularity; and justice requires either that the case should be sent back for a re-hearing or reconsideration, as a whole, upon the pleadings and proofs, to enable the Court to make one complete decree covering all branches of the case—which we must assume would be the same in effect as the two which we now have; or we should overlook the irregularity, if it be one, and treat the case as now before us upon both decrees, as one. I think the latter the true course, and that it would be idle ceremony and gross injustice to the appellee to send it back.

We proceed, therefore, to the consideration of the case upon its merits.

The first question arises upon the validity of the restraining clause in the contract.

It is objected that this is void; and upon this ground defendant, Chase, while retaining the large consideration that was paid him for the property and business deliberately proposed to disregard his promises, and the other defendants joined him in his attempt to build up a business that must depend for its success on the substantial destruction of that which Chase had sold and been paid for, and which he had agreed not to compete with. And this objection presents for our consideration the principle point in the case, and the one to which counsel directed their chief attention.

The precise ground of supposed invalidity is that the contract imposed upon Chase a general restraint of trade; and this, it is said, is void by the ancient common law of England, fully accepted and universally followed in this country. The restraint consisted in his binding himself not to engage in the printing and publishing business anywhere in the State of Michigan, while Beal should continue to carry on at Ann Arbor the business which was the subject of the contract. The invalidity is supposed to be shown by a great number of authorities to which our attention has been called, beginning with *Mitchell v. Reynolds 1 V. Wm. 181* (1 Smith Leading Cases, 172) where the doctrine relied upon first finds distinct expression. That case was debt upon a bond, conditioned that the defendant should not exercise the trade of a baker within a certain parish for the term of five years; and Chief Justice Parker in delivering the opinion of the Court, while holding the bond good, and the restraint upon trade to the extent imposed by it perfectly legal and unobjectionable, provided it was based upon sufficient consideration, went beyond the case to a general discussion of restraint of trade, and laid down rules which, though quite unnecessary in the particular controversy, have with some modifications and qualifications been accepted as law and followed from that time to the present. All general restraints upon trade he held to be void; and a restraint was said to be general within the meaning of the law, which extended to the whole kingdom. Apparently regarding all contracts in restraint of trade presumptively illegal, he nevertheless classifies them as follows: "Where the restraint is general not to exercise a trade throughout the kingdom and where it is limited to a particular place, for the former of these must be void being of no benefit to either party, and only oppressive, shall be shown bye and bye;" p. 182. And again he says such a restraint could "be of no use to the obligee; which holds in all cases of general restraint throughout England, for what does it signify to a tradesman in London what another does in Newcastle? and surely it would be unreasonable to fix a certain law on one side without any benefit to the other. The Roman Law would not enforce such contracts by an action." The ground of the invalidity, then seems to be the impossibility that so broad a restraint could be of the least use or benefit to the party imposing it, in which case it is perfectly correct to speak of the contract as wholly oppressive, and in so far as it tended to deprive the public of the benefit that might be conferred by the labor and skill of a citizen, it would be contrary to public policy. Again the learned Justice says, "There is more than a presumption against it, *because it can never be useful to any man to restrain another from trading in all places;* though it may be to restrain him trading in some, unless he intends a monopoly, which is a crime,' p. 193. And in conclusion he says, "In all restraints of trade where nothing more appears, the law presumes them bad; but if the circumstances are set forth, that presumption is excluded, and the Court is to judge of those circumstances, and determine accordingly; and if upon them it appears to be a just and honest contract it ought to be maintained," p. 197.

This case is the foundation of the rule relied upon; and the dictum of the learned Judge most unequivocally shows that the reason for his opinion that a restraint coextensive with the kingdom would be void, was the impossibility that one man could have an interest in a restraint so broad upon the trade of another. This decision was made more than a century and a half ago—and for a condition of things and a state of society wholly different from those which now prevail. It may have been quite true at that time that to a person following any particular trade, profession or occupation in London, it would be wholly immaterial whether any other person was or was not following the same trade, profession or occupation in Newcastle, since the little business intercourse and the difficulty and delay of communication would wholly preclude anything like competition between two persons in the same occupation thus circumstanced. But it cannot be said that the same fact is true any longer in England, or that it could be true of the State of Michigan to-day. In some occupations it is well known that rivalry and competition are active between professional men, artisans and merchants, located at extreme points, and that in some cases this competition may be quite as severe and effective at a distant point as in the same locality where another is located. Indeed in some cases where a single house is competent to supply all the demands of a State in its line, or when one manufactory would be fully equal to all its wants, the one establishment would not only have an interest in keeping out any other, but it would be interested to the whole value of its business, which the competition might render utterly worthless. If, therefore, we look only to the interests of the parties contracting, there would seem to be nothing in the reasons assigned, by Chief Justice Parker, which should necessarily preclude a contract as broad as the one here disputed, provided the proper interest appeared to support it.

It is said, however, that the public is a third party in such cases, and that the public is concerned to prevent such contracts because:

1. They tend to prevent competition, which the public interest favors, and

2. They deprive the State of the services of a citizen by binding him to idleness or emigration.

As to the first ground it may be said it is quite true the public are interested in competition in business; but this is not true under all circumstances nor to every extent. The public is quite as much interested in the prosperity of its citizens in their various avocations as it can possibly be in their competition. The latter may bring low prices to purchasers, but may also bring them so low that capital becomes unprofitable and business men fail, to the general injury of the community. If only one publishing house of large capital could be prosperous in the county of Washtenaw, the people of the county can have no interest in the investment of large capital in a second, and the sharper the competition the more unfortunate for the people, it ruin to the parties concerned must result. The illustration holds good for the State when the particular busines competed with is of State interest and importance,for no community can be benefited by the competition of its members where it is carried beyond the bounds of a reasonable prosperity to the parties engaged in it. This is fully recognized by Chief Justice Parker in *Mitchell vs. Reynolds*, who assigns as one reason which may support contracts in restraint of trade, "that there may happen instances wherein they may be useful and beneficial, *as to prevent a town from being overstocked with any particular trade;* or in case of an old man, who finding himself under such circumstances, either of body or mind, as that he is likely to be a loser by continuing his trade; in this case it will be better for him to part with it for a consideration, that by selling his custom he may procure to himself a livelihood which he might probably have lost by trading longer." p. 190. If then their tendency to preclude competition may be a reason for denying validity to such contracts in some cases, their preventing it seems to have been found a sufficient reason for upholding them in others; so that competition seems not to be regarded as necessarily in itself beneficial, but as something which may or may not be beneficial according to the circumstances. And it may well be asked who in general are the best judges of these circumstances; the parties concerned who have an interest in making them the subject of their contracts, or the Courts who can obtain of the circumstances only such partial and unsatisfactory views as conflicting and imperfect evidence can give them?

As to the second ground it must be conceded that the State has always an interest that none of its citizens shall be kept in enforced idleness. But when a contract only binds a person not to engage in a particular business within the State, is this consequence a necessary or even a probable one? It certainly might have been so in England in the days of Chief Justice Parker, when a system of apprenticeship prevailed which rendered it exceedingly difficult for one to obtain a living by his industry in any other avocation than that for which he had fitted himself by serving his time under its rules and under the law, but in this country at this time where a change of occupation is too common to excite remark; where merchants become manufacturers, and lawyers farmers, and farmers traders, not because they receive a consideration for doing so, but because with larger opportunities for observation than they had at first, they have fully satisfied themselves that such changes will be for their advantage, as oftentimes they prove to be—any rule of law which should assume that one who for a consideration bargains not to follow his previous business, had thereby bound himself to idleness and penury, to the detriment of the State, *would be a rule absurd in itself*, and contrary to general experience and observation. On the contrary, where such a contract is the result of fair bargaining, the reasonable presumption is that each party, in view of all the circumstances which were within his own intimate knowledge, was able to see how the bargain was to result to his advantage, and that the party resigning the business did not do so without being fully satisfied that he was receiving full equivalent, which would be more advantageous to him than the property and the business sold. And where a man has fully decided to sell his business to take up another, can there be any reason of state policy why he should be precluded from bargaining for the additional consideration he can obtain by agreeing not to engage in the same business? If a man can sell his business for ten thousand dollars only, but the purchaser will give twice as much in case the seller will agree not to engage in a ruinous competition with him, what interest has the public in denying to the seller the right of selling for this additional sum, or in releasing him from his bargain, if after he has received it, *he shall coolly repudiate* this portion of his contract, while he keeps the consideration he has received for it. If there be any sufficient reason, it was not presented on the argument, and it is not hinted at in any of the cases to which our attention has been directed.

And it certainly can be no sufficient objection to such a contract that it may possibly result in one party going beyond the *State limits* to engage in the same business anew. What if it shall do so? Are our interests as a State so petty or exclusive and our policy so narrow and invidious that we frame rules to keep people within the State contrary to their inclination, or when it would be for their interest to go elsewhere? *Yet this narrow, illiberal* and exclusive policy must certainly be relied upon, if the tendency of a contract to induce a contracting party to leave the State is to defeat the contract. If such a position is sound, then a contract made in this State for the services of a citizen at Chicago, or any other point outside the State, should be treated as void here, because depriving the State of the benefit that might flow from the industry of one of its citizens! Or to take a case still more exactly parallel: Partners in trade at *Superior City* might divide their stock, and one for a consideration, agrees that he would remove his share across the river to Duluth, and not again engage in the business at Superior City; but this agreement, though perfectly reasonable, considered with reference to the individuals only, would on this doctrine be void, because a *State policy which has come down to us from a semi-civilized or less enlightened times, when governments were accustomed to prohibit artisans from leaving the realm, and gold and silver from being exported, is supposed to be violated by the transfer of the industry and capital of a citizen across a river into another State. The position seems to us to require no further attention.*

It may be well now to examine some of the later cases to see if they have enlarged the reasons upon which the rule of law relied upon by the defendants was originally rested. In *Davis v. Mason, 5 T.R., 120,* Lord Kenyon in sustaining an argument restraining one from practicing as a surgeon within ten miles of a certain town, dismissed the objection that it restricted competition by saying that the public were not likely to be injured by an agreement of this kind, since every other person was at liberty to practice as a surgeon in the town. In *Howe v. Ashford, 3 Bing. 326, Best Ch. J.,* in passing upon a contract of partial restraint says: "The law will not permit any one to restrain a person from doing what the public welfare and his own interest requires that he should do. Any deed, therefore, by which a person binds himself not to employ his talents, his industry or his capital in any useful undertaking in the kingdom would be void, *because no good reason can be imagined for any person imposing such a restraint on himself*. But it may often happen (and the present case is a strong instance of it), that individual interest and general convenience render engagements not to carry on trades or to act in a profession, in a particular place proper. Manufactures or dealings cannot be carried on to any great extent without the assistance of agents and servants. These must soon acquire a knowledge of the manufactures or dealings of their employers. A merchant or manufacturer would soon find a rival in every one of his servants if he could not prevent them from using to his prejudice the knowledge acquired in his employ.

Engagements of this sort between masters and servants are not injurious restraints of trade, but securities necessary for those who are engaged in it. The effect of such contracts is to encourage rather than to cramp the employment of capital in trade, and the promotion of industry." Here is the same recognition of the fact that competition is sometimes injurious, which we find in *Mitchell v. Reynolds,* and here also we see that the public interest which is to render the contract void is not any general public interest irrespective of the interest of the parties, but an interest that no one shall be restrained in his own proper action where benefit can possibly result to no one from the restraint.

In *Homer v. Graves, 7 Bing. 735,* an agreement that a moderately skilled dentist would abstain from practicing over a district 200 miles in diameter, was held void on the express ground that the extent of territory covered by it was beyond what, in view of the local character of the business, could be reasonable. And Tindall, Ch. J., said: "We do not see how a better test can be applied to the question, whether reasonable or not, than by considering whether the restraint is such only as to afford a fair protection to the interest of the party in favor of whom it is given, and not so large as to interfere with the interests of the public. Whatever restraint is larger than the necessary protection of the party can be of no benefit to either, it can only be oppressive; and if oppressive, it is in the eye of the law unreasonable.

No precise boundary can be laid down within which the restraint would be reasonable, and beyond which excessive." In *Ward v. Byrne, 5 M. & W. 547.* The rule by which all the

Court proposed to try the reasonableness of a restraint upon trade, was whether it was only co-extensive with the interests of the person with whom the contract was made. In *Wallace v. May*, 11 M. & W. 667, a contract excluding a dentist from practice in the city of London, then containing a population equal to more than two-thirds that of this State now, was sustained, the Court again measuring its reasonableness by the interest of the party contracting for the restriction, and declaring that "it would be better to lay down such a limit as under any circumstances, would be sufficient protection to the interests of the contracting party, and if the limit stipulated for does not exceed that, to pronounce the contract to be valid." How this can be reconciled with a rule which under all circumstances would confine the restriction within the limits of State boundaries it is impossible for us to understand. Such boundaries have little or no relation to the range of many kinds of business; for trade heeds not the mathematical lines by which State limits are indicated, but follows everywhere the law of demand and supply, unless unfriendly statutes interpose.

Lord Langdale in *Whittaker v. Howe, 3 Beav.*, 383, expressly repudiated the doctrine that a general restriction extending to the whole kingdom, was to be held under all circumstances unreasonable. The contract in question imposed upon attorneys and solicitors who had sold their business, a general restraint from taking it up again. This learned Judge treated the question involved as one of reasonableness, considered from the standpoint of the contracting parties; and declaring his concurence with the Court of Common Pleas in *Homer v. Graves*, that in such cases no precise boundary could be laid down, but the circumstances of the particular case must determine it, he accepted and adopted the words of Lord Kenyon in *Davis v. Mason*, 4 T. & R. 118. "I do not see that the limits are necessarily unreasonable, nor do I know how to draw the line." An injunction was therefore awarded to restrain a breach of the agreement.

Some question has been raised upon the case of *Whittaker v Howe*, and it is said it cannot stand with the other authorities. If those which declare a restriction co-extensive with the State are to be understood as laying down an inflexible rule, then it certainly cannot stand with them; but if they are to be understood as giving only an illustration which in most cases will sufficiently indicate the unreasonableness of a restraint, then it may well stand with them, if the reasons upon which it is based are the same which other cases have applied to different circumstances. And that the reasons are precisely the same has already been seen. Those reasons were applied again by Lord Campbell in *Fallis v. Fallis*, 1 El. & Bl., 391. 18 E. L. & E., 151, in which a covenant not to engage in the book canvassing trade in London, or within 120 miles of the General Post Office, nor in Dublin or Edinburgh, or within 50 miles of either, nor in any town in Great Britain or Ireland in which the covenantee or his successors might at any time have an establishment, or might have had one for six months preceding, was held not to be unreasonable. Here was a restriction which, considering the territory covered by it, was more extensive than that which these defendants question; and considering the population to be supplied was many times as extensive, and the business was analogous to that which was here restrained. Would it not, therefore, be absurd to say that the restriction in this case must be considered unreasonable, because it embraced the whole State, but that the one in that case must be held reasonable because certain corners of a much more extensive and populous country might possibly be left open to occupancy by the covenantor? Lord Campbell, reviewing the earlier authorities, justly remarks that "the law relating to contracts in restraint of trade has been altered by late decisions; and that, while in *Mitchell v. Reynolds*, they were held *prima facie* bad; according to the tenor of the later decisions the contract is valid unless some restriction is imposed beyond what the interest of plaintiff requires; and his interest has been considered to extend very widely."

And he makes remarks in the case which apply with great force to the defendant in this case. Chase, who having obtained a large sum on the sale of a business which he represented as extending to the whole State and much beyond it, now turns around, and on evidence that his representations were too large, and on the pretence of regard for some principle of State policy, which is to be subserved by his breach of contract *seeks to retain the consideration while repudiating the promise on which he obtained it*. "*The facts of the case,*" he says "are strong to show that the general rule may be well applied in respect to the present defence. The defendant * * * was probably acquainted with the business to which the covenant relates. He stipulated for, and obtained a large price for consenting to the restriction; and as far as we can perceive, he is endeavoring to keep that price without making the return for which it was paid; and he is attempting to support this proceeding on the ground that the public interest would be sacrificed, if his publications are not brought out. *It is clear that there would be evil if the law justified such a breach of contract*. but it is by no means clear there would be any compensating good to the public from the publications intended by the defendant to be so made in violation of his promise to the plaintiff."

The true rule, it seems to us, is laid down with great clearness and accuracy by the Vice Chancellor in *Leather Cloth Co. v. Lorsont*, Law R. 9 Eq. 345, 353, in which, referring to the argument that a general restraint, extending to the whole kingdom is on its face bad. he says: "I do not read the cases as having laid down that unrebuttable presumption which was insisted upon with so much power by (counsel). All the cases when they come to be examined seem to establish this principle: that all restraints upon trade are bad, as being in violation of public policy, unless they are natural and not unreasonable for the protection of the parties in dealing legally with some subject matter of contract. The principle is this: public policy requires that every man shall be at liberty to work for himself, and shall not be at liberty to deprive himself or the State of his labor, skill or talent, by any contract that he enters into. On the other hand, public policy requires that when a man has by skill or by any other means attained something which he wants to sell, *he should be at liberty to sell it* in the most advantageous way in the market; and in order to enable him to sell it advantageously in the market, it is necessary that he should *be able to preclude himself from entering into competition with the purchaser*. In such a case the same public policy that enables him to do that, does not restrain him from alienating that which he wants to alienate, and therefore enables him to enter into any stipulation, however restrictive it is, provided that restriction, in the judgment of the court, is not unreasonable, having regard to the subject matter of the contract." Precisely the same rule is laid down in *Morse Twist Drill and Machine Co. v. Morse*, 103 Mass. 73. 77, which was the case of a restriction not confined within any territorial limits, and in which other recent English cases to the same effect are referred to. And Chapman, Ch. J., well remarks: "In this country there are periodical publications that have a very wide circulation, and it is obvious that a purchaser of the proprietorship cannot afford to pay the full value, unless he can obtain from the vendor a valid restriction against competition, which restriction shall be as extensive as his interest requires, *though it may cover the whole of a State, or the whole country*. The same would be true as to some books. For example, the author of a popular school book could not sell its proprietorship for its full value unless he could bind himself not to prepare another book which should be used in competition with it. The same would be true as to some manufactured articles. The present case furnishes an illustration. The defendant could not have obtained the consideration which was paid him if it had been understood that this contract which he has violated had no validity. *He is appropriating to himself a part of that which he has sold to the plaintiff*, and which is valuable property to them." And the same general view was taken by the Supreme Court of the United States in *Oregon Steam Navigation Co. v. Winsor, Wal.*, in which it was expressly declared that the State limits are no tests of the reasonableness of a contract in restraint of trade, and that much latitude must be allowed to the judgment and discretion of parties who bargain for the restraint in view and with an intimate knowledge of their own business interests. And a restraint was held valid in that case, though it embraced the whole territory of a State and even more than that.

We do not deem it important to examine the cases further in detail. It is manifest that if it could fairly be regarded for the interest of Chase, when he made this contract, to consent to this restriction, because of a greater ability to sell at a good price if he would do so, and for the interest of Beal to insist upon it, because it would protect him against the competition of Chase and give him a more reasonable prospect of business success, *then the restriction* CANNOT BE HELD VOID WITHOUT DISREGARDING ALL THE AUTHORITIES WHICH REST UPON *any* SOUND *principle. And we think there is every* REASON for holding that presumptively it was for the interest of both parties to agree upon the restriction which was expressed in their contract. The one made a sale for a greater price by this means, and the other *protected himself against a competition* which the evidence in this case shows might easily have become *ruinous*.

And the best possible evidence that it was *for the interest of both parties to make the contract, is, that they deliberately made it,* and probably at the time with the full intention of observing it. Certain it is that it was faithfully kept for a time. What induced Chase afterwards to advance step by step, in its violation, it is needless to speculate; we have only to determine whether *his conduct was in disregard of the law; and we are clearly of the opinion that it was*. And we are also of opinion that in view of his representations and his contract, he is estopped from denying that the business he sold was co-extensive with the State. *That the defendant corporation is liable to complainant to the full extent that Chase is, would seem to be clear,* unless the fact that Krause testifies to an ignorance of the contract on his part when he became a corporator, should be found an important circumstance. The other corporators knew about the contract, consulted about it, made up their minds it could not be enforced, and deliberately concluded to take the risk. They cannot complain, therefore, if having thus voluntarily participated with Chase *in a deliberate injury to the complainant's business, they are left to share with him the consequences.* Had defendants constituted a partnership instead of a corporation the joint responsibility of all would have been clear, and notice of the contract to one would have been notice to all. It is insisted, however, that no such rule can be applied to corporators, and the absurdity of holding a railroad corporation, for instance, chargeable with notice of anything that may be known by any persons who may buy a share of its stock, is forcibly pressed upon our attention. Such a case has little if any analogy to the present. This is the case of six men who unite in a business usually carried on by partners, who meet and consult, and talk over their plans as partners are accustomed to do, but who avail themselves of a corporate organization, not as a necessity, but as a possible convenience. Among the things talked over, and *probably the most important of all, is the existence of this contract. All but one admit it to have been the subject of their consultations,* and if Chase failed to apprise that one of it, we can only say he was wanting in that good faith to an associate which was obviously incumbent upon him. Now it is not denied that had the organization assumed the form of a partnership, Krause would have been charged with constructive notice. To hold that he is not so charged because, for the convenience of the business, the organization was made to assume a corporate form, is to base an important distinction on what seems to us a wholly immaterial circumstance.

The probability that Krause would have notice in fact is the same in the one case as in the other, and the reason why the association thus formed for a violation of the contract with complainant should respond for the consequences, are not varied in the slightest degree by its taking on a corporate form rather than any other.

If Krause had innocently bought into the business afterwards, some other considerations would need to be discussed; but he was one of the original associates. The stock all remained in the hands of the original subscribers when the injury to complainant was committed, and it seems to us a manifest absurdity to hold that *the neglect of his associates to lay before him a fact so important to their enterprise, when good faith to him required that they should do so, should protect the association against the consequences of this deliberate violation of contract rights.* Not assuming to lay down any general rule, but confining what we have to say to the precise facts of this case, *we are of opinion that this corporation is and ought to be jointly responsible with Chase.*

The defendants also insist that complainant lost his right to proceed against them by laches in commencing suit. Laches is a most important circumstance where parties are proceeding to expend money in reliance upon a supposed right, and upon the apparent acquiescence of the party who might question the right. But in this case defendants were misled by no acquiescence. They entered upon their undertaking in open and known hostility to the complainant, and in reliance, not upon his acquiescence, *but upon their ability to defeat him in a legal contest.* They knew from the very first that their position in respect to this contract must be antagonistic to that of complainant, and no consideration of good faith on his part could require that he should open the legal warfare at the very earliest opportunity. When a hostile attitude is thus taken, the challenged party may justly be expected and reasonably be allowed to be wary and deliberate in choosing his time and opportunity for attack. The delay in filing the present bill was less than a year from the organization of the corporation, and in the mean time a bill on a collateral branch of the controversy had been filed and important action taken upon it. It is impossible, therefore, to hold complainant guilty of any laches which these defendants are in position to complain of. He might have moved sooner; but the law does not demand the utmost exertion of diligence in repelling a hostile invasion of one's rights thus deliberately taken with full knowledge of all the facts.

It is denied by defendants that the Court had any power to award damages in the case; the question of damages being, they insist, peculiarly one for the consideration of courts of law. In support of this position a number of English cases are cited, in some of which, decided since Lord Cairns' Act (21 and 22 Victoria), which expressly authorized the court of chancery to give compensation in damages in some cases, it has been stated by the court that previous to that act chancery had no power to award damages. Whether these statements were meant to be understood literally, or whether on the other hand they were intended to be understood only as statements that previous to that statute the court had no power to grant relief in damages when no other relief was given, is not very clear, and perhaps not very important. Relief was certainly given in some cases in the English court of chancery by an award of damages, previous to the passage of that act; and there are decisions which even go so far as to hold that damages might be awarded in cases of specific performance, even though the principal relief sought was denied. The leading case of *Denton v. Stuart*, 1 Cox. 253 referred to in 1 Toub Eq. 43 et s q., which holds this doctrine is overruled in England, the Master of the Rolls holding in *Greanaway v. Adams*, 12 Ves. 401, that where specific relief was denied, either because improper under the facts, or because it was impracticable, there was no basis for any relief in damages, and the party must be turned over to his remedy at law. See also *Todd v. Gee*, 17 Ves. 273. *Denton v. Stuart* has sometimes been followed in this country. See *Andrews v. Brown* 3 Cush 134; *Phillips v. Thompson*, 1 Johns. Ch. 150; but Chancellor Kent declined to follow his own decision subsequently, holding in *Hatch v. Cobb*, 4 Johns. Ch. 559 and again in *Kempshell v. Stone*, 5 Johns. Ch. 193, that the court ought not, except in very special cases, to sustain a bill for the award of damages merely. But in neither of these cases was the authority of the court, after granting the principal relief, to award damages, where it was necessary to do complete justice between the parties, denied or questioned; and its right, and indeed its duty to do so, instead of turning the parties over to a second litigation, has often been declared in this country, in reliance upon what was believed to be the settled rule in England irrespective of any statute. And the cases are by no means confined, as was argued by counsel, to those in which the award of damages would consist in an adjudication as to profits; but most of them are cases of specific performance where the plaintiff established his right, but the defendant was unable to perform fully, or perhaps, after suit brought, had disabled himself from performing at all.

The right of the court to award incidental compensation where its jurisdiction is made out, is not, however, by these cases made to depend on the nature of the principal relief, but on the fact that the parties being properly before the court for one purpose, complete justice can be more easily, speedily and inexpensively done between them as to all the matters embraced in the suit, by the adjudication of the court of chancery being made to embrace them all, than by a decree as to a part which dismisses the case with a view to a suit at law as to the remainder. See *King v. Baueau*, 6 Johns. Ch. 38; *Wiswall v. McGowan*, 1 Hoff. 125; Same case on appeal. 2 Barb. 270; *Cathcart v. Robinson*, 5 Ret. 263; *Climie v. Heale*, 1 Munf. 63; *Turner v. Layton*, cited in 1 Ohio, 130; *Gibbs v. Champion*, 3 Ohio, 337; *Williams v. Champion*, 6 Ohio, 170; *Dustin v. Newcomer*, 8 Ohio. 49; *Jones v. Harrison*, 3 Heyw. 92; *Slaughter v. Tindle*, 1 Litt. 338; *White v. Hardin*, 5 Dana, 141; *Watham v. Aldham*. 9 Dana, 50; *Chapman v. M. R. & L. E. R. R. Co.*, 6 Ohio, N. S. 119; *Doggath v. Hart*, 5 Flor. 215; *Martin v. Tidwell*, 36 Ga 332; *Brown v. Gardner*, Har. Ch. 291; *Carrol v. Rice*, Walker's Ch. 273. These cases and numerous others in which the same doctrine is incidentally recognized, were the warrant of the Circuit Court in giving complete relief in the case.

We now come to the question of the correspondence.

What is the fair meaning and extent of the covenant at the close of the contract, that "said Beal is to have the privilege of receiving the letters connected with said business, and opening the same"? This can only be understood by reference to the subject matter and the surrounding circumstances to which the covenant relates, the nature of the "said" business, the mode in which it was carried on, or was expected to be carried on, as well as the nature of the correspondence and its connection with the business.

Chase had, by the same instrument, conveyed to Beal the whole printing, binding and publishing establishment and business, the First Receipt Book, the publication and sale of which constituted the principal source of profit and inducement to the purchase, the newspaper he was publishing, with its subscription list, and his right to two other books, together with the good will of the business of printing and publishing, and the right to use the name of Chase in connection with said book and the publishing business, giving him also the right to carry on the whole business transferred, under the name of "Dr. Chase's Steam Printing House," and had required Beal to fulfil all contracts previously entered into by Chase. The correspondence had been and was mainly in reference to the Receipt Book and its sale, letters transmitting orders for the book and remittances in various forms to pay for it, as well as orders for work to be done in printing and binding. These letters, like the few Chase had been receiving which did not relate to the business, had nothing upon the outside to indicate whether they related to the business, or were private, or merely personal, having no reference to the business. Those thus directed, however, which did not relate to the business were extremely few in comparison with those which did—not more than one in five hundred, if more than one in a thousand. Until opened it could not be known whether any particular letter was of the one class or the other, though the chances were five hundred or a thousand to one that they related to the business sold to Beal, and therefore belonged to him. One party or the other must have the right to open them and determine their character (unless some third person was agreed upon, which was not done). This right was therefore very properly and necessarily given to Beal, who had so much the greater interest, and without which he could not safely carry on the business he had purchased. And though the contract does not express it in so many words, no one can doubt that the fair implication arising from this contract would be that if Beal on opening any letter should find it did not relate to the business he had purchased, but to Chase personally, it would be his duty to hand it to Chase, or give it the proper directions to reach him. And it is entirely obvious also that Chase had it in his own power, and would naturally, like any other prudent man under like circumstances, take a private box, and notify most if not all his personal or private correspondents to address their letters to this box, or give the number of his residence, or in some other way to denote that it was intended for him personally; and this we accordingly find was precisely what he did.

In view of these considerations, I think it entirely clear that the order and directions given to the postmaster immediately after the sale, in reference to the delivery of the correspondence to Beal and his right to take the same and its contents, to sign and receipt for these same in Chase's name, was no more than the fair result and just interpretation of the covenant in his own contract with Beal, and no more than by his contract he was bound to do. I cannot, therefore, consider it, as contended by the defendants, a mere voluntary license given by Chase, and to be revoked at his pleasure, nor even a new verbal contract, but a part and a very essential part of the property rights conveyed by Chase to Beal, which he had no more right to revoke than he had to revoke the sale of the printing presses or the real estate sold at the same time, and as a part of the same transaction.

It seems to me, therefore, clear, whatever view might be taken of any other question in the case, that the complainant is entitled to a decree for carrying this portion of the contract into full effect, and to an injunction restraining Chase and all persons acting or claiming to act under his authority, from taking such correspondence from the postoffice. The decree as rendered in the Court below ought to be slightly modified in this regard, so that the injunction shall not restrain or prohibit Chase from receiving from the postoffice such letters coming or to come to this office to his address, as may have upon the outside or envelope the number of his residence or any other mark or word clearly indicating that the same is intended for Chase personally, unconnected with the business sold to Beal, as well as those having upon them the number of his private postoffice box, with the further provision, however, as a part of this modification, and upon the same principle that a decree for the execution of a deed or release is granted by courts of equity, that the defendant Chase should be decreed to execute and deliver to Beal a written order, directed to the postmaster, requesting him to deliver all such correspondence (not specially addressed in one of the three modes just above indicated), authorizing Beal to receipt for the same and for any of the contents, and to sign Chase's name to any proper receipt to the postmaster for money, drafts, registered letters, postoffice money orders, and other remittances enclosed in or pertaining to any such correspondence in reference to the business so sold to Beal; but such written order to the postmaster expressly to except all letters addressed to Chase having on the outside or envelope the number of his private postoffice box, or the number of his residence, or any other mark or word clearly indicating that such letter is intended for Chase personally, or that it is not connected with the business so sold to Beal. In all other respects the decree of the Court below should be affirmed, and the complainant should recover his costs in both Courts.

(Signed)
I. P. CHRISTIANCY.

DECISION OF THE SUPREME COURT.

Rendered Tuesday, April 27, 1875.

Rice A. Beal
vs.
Alvan W. Chase and the Ann Arbor Printing and Publishing Company.

In this case there have been two appeals taken. The last one was from a decree taken while the former was pending in this Court, and was made as an additional decree upon no new hearing, and upon the case as presented to the Circuit Court when the first decree was made. As the statute expressly declares that on a chancery appeal, "All proceedings shall be stayed, until otherwise ordered by the Supreme Court" (C. L. §5181), a majority of us think that the Circuit Court had no power to make the second decree, and that it should be reversed, but without costs, as the return was not duplicated and the second decree was made on the Judge's own motion. We do not discuss the questions covered by it.

Upon the first decree the Court has arrived at a substantial agreement, although not agreeing in all respects, in the reasons on which their action will be based. They will content themselves with as brief a reference as will make their views intelligible.

The bill was filed to restrain the alleged violation, or rights secured to complainant in connection with, a sale to him by defendant Chase of a printing and publishing business and certain copyrights. Chase had built up a large and prosperous business in Ann Arbor, known very generally throughout the state and having a widely extended custom, under the name of "Dr. Chase's Steam Printing House." He had also published a very popular Recipe Book which was circulated largely by means of correspondence and agencies, as well as advertising, and brought in large profits. For a large and adequate consideration Chase sold to Beal his whole establishment, including a newspaper, the Recipe Book, and other copyrights, "together with the good will of the business, of printing and publishing, and also the right to use the name of Dr. Chase, in connection with said books; and providing that the said Beal, on his part, if he chooses, may carry on said business, and shall have the exclusive right, under the name of 'Dr. Chase's Steam Printing House,' and may add R. A. Beal, proprietor." The accounts were also transferred, and some other things not important here. The following important provisions are directly involved in this controversy: Chase agreed not to engage directly or indirectly "in the business of printing and publishing in the state of Michigan" so long as Beal should remain in the business of printing and publishing in the city of Ann Arbor. Beal was also "to have the privilege of receiving the letters connected with said business and opening the same." This was in August, 1869. Chase left Ann Arbor not many months thereafter, and was absent some time in another residence in the West. Just after the sale he gave Beal authority to take from the postoffice all letters not directed to his private box, and to obtain and receipt for all remittances and orders for money. Beal continued in a prosperous business and unmolested, until the course of action complained of began in 1872.

Chase during that year having conceived the opinion that his contract was void, as an undue restraint of trade, began preparation for a new printing business, and began to prepare a new Receipt Book, and revoked his authority to Beal to obtain the letters not addressed to the Printing House.

In August, 1872, several persons who had been thinking of setting up a Printing establishment, but who had done nothing, negotiated with Chase, the result of which was the formation of the defendant corporation, with a nominal capital of $50,000, of which Chase took one-half. They immediately began a general Printing and Publishing business, and started a newspaper, and became formidable rivals of Beal. Dr. Chase became, and was announced conspicuously as their President and Business Manager. He prepared a New Receipt Book which was called Dr. Chase's Second Receipt Book, and which purported to include receipts on many subjects covering similar ground with the first, but more extensive and higher-priced. Vigorous efforts were made to circulate it, as superior to the first, and it was brought directly to the attention of persons who had dealt in or purchased the first. For this purpose use was made of correspondence intended for the publisher of the first book, and persons writing for that were informed of the publication, and impressed with the superiority, of the Second Book.

Beal filed a bill in 1872 to restrain the publication of this Second Book, which the Ann Arbor Printing and Publishing Company had made an agreement to publish on a royalty. In July, 1873, the present bill was filed, complaining of all the acts above mentioned.

After suit was brought Chase sold out his stock, and retired from the Company, and the publication of the Second Receipt Book was removed to Toledo.

The final decree enjoined Chase from being engaged directly or indirectly in the Printing and Publishing business in this State, or printing or publishing the Second Receipt Book in this State, and from taking or opening any letters relating to Dr. Chase's Recipes or Chase's Steam Printing House. The defendant corporation was enjoined from doing said business with or for Chase, directly or indirectly.

We are all agreed that Chase's connection with the business of the defendant Company was such as to be a direct violation of his contract, and that the Company knew of the contract throughout. We are all agreed that the measures taken to get a circulation of the New Receipt Book, by the agencies and correspondence which had been or were at any time used or designed for the first, were unlawful. We are all agreed that Beal was entitled to all correspondence intended for the old establishment, and first Recipe Book, and that in case of doubt, he was entitled to the benefit of the doubt as to its being so intended.

We are all agreed that Chase had no right to publish by the terms of that contract in Michigan (if valid,) any Receipt Book so connected with his name as to lead to the inference that it was designed to supersede the old one. And we concur (with some doubt on the part of one of us) that the New Receipt Book with its title and announcements has that tendency.

Concerning the validity of the agreement, we concur in regarding it as not unreasonable in fact, and as based on full consideration. One of us has doubted, whether it could properly include the whole State, but considering the rule to the contrary as somewhat artificial, he concurs in maintaining the agreement.

Although some questions might arise as to whether a corporation could be restrained from dealings prohibited to a stockholder, merely because it had such a stockholder, we do not discuss that, because Chase's connection with this Company was something more; and the terms of the decree cannot fairly be wrested into any unreasonable meaning.

Our conclusion is that the first decree should be affirmed with costs, leaving questions of damages to be determined at law, and directing a power or authority to be executed whereby Beal can obtain the letters belonging to him and making such modifications as are necessary to that end, and until such authority is executed, that the decree stand as equivalent thereto and may be used to obtain such letters from the Post Office.

(Signed)　　　　　J. V. CAMPBELL.
　　　　　　　　　T. M. COOLEY.
　　　　　　　　　B. F. GRAVES.

FINAL DECREE IN THE SUPREME COURT.

At a session of the Supreme Court of the State of Michigan, held at the Supreme Court Room in the City of Lansing, on the twenty-seventh day of April in the year one thousand eight hundred and seventy-five.

Present, the Hon. BENJAMIN F. GRAVES, Chief Justice.

THOMAS M. COOLEY, JAMES V. CAMPBELL, ISAAC MARSTON, Associate Justices.

Rice A. Beal, Complainant
vs.
Alvan W. Chase and the Ann Arbor Printing and Publishing Company, Defendants.

This cause having been heard and considered upon the two separate appeals taken therein, it is now ordered, adjudged and decreed that the last decree made therein by the Circuit Court for the County of Washtenaw was erroneous by reason of the pendency of an appeal in this Court from the former decree whereby the authority of said Circuit Court to proceed was suspended until the further order of this Court; and the said last decree is therefore reversed and vacated but without costs to either party.

And it is further ordered, adjudged and decreed that the decree of the said Circuit Court first made and appealed from, to wit, the decree of June 1st, 1874 be and the same is in all things affirmed except as to those matters which were therein reserved for further decision, and as to those matters it is ordered and adjudged that no further proceedings be had in equity and that the question of damages be left to such action or actions as the Complainant may see fit to bring at law; and as to the correspondence mentioned in the pleadings in this cause and in said decree it is ordered and adjudged that the Complainant is lawfully entitled to receive directly and the said Chase shall continue to be enjoined against interfering with all correspondence coming to the Postoffice in Ann Arbor which is directed to the defendant Chase and which does not indicate by the direction or other plain indications that it does not relate to the business or to the Receipt Book which the Complainant purchased from said Chase under the contract set forth in the Bill of Complaint, and that said Complainant is entitled to receive and appropriate all sums of money and all other valuable enclosures contained in such correspondence, restoring to the said Chase without delay any correspondence and enclosures which upon opening, the same shall appear to belong to said Chase and not to said Complainant. And it is further ordered, adjudged, and decreed that the said Chase do without delay execute to said Beal an irrevocable power of attorney to receive such correspondence from the Postoffice, and to receipt for and endorse any remittances, drafts, money orders or other valuable enclosures which may be contained in or accompany the same, and that this decree shall stand operative as such authority in all respects until such power is executed and delivered to said Beal. And it is further ordered adjudged and decreed that said Complainant recover of said Defendants his costs in this Court of said first appeal to be taxed and that he have execution therefor, and that this cause be remanded to the Circuit Court for the County of Washtenaw for any further proceedings under this decree.

AN EDITORIAL.

The following Editorial appeared in the Peninsular Courier of April 30, 1875:

In this issue of our paper will be found the opinion in brief of the Supreme Court of this State, in the above named cause. The struggle is now at last ended, and our friends can rejoice with us, while our enemies and opponents *must weep*. The conflict has been one of unusual length and interest. It was not only of vital interest to us, but we believe it has been of interest and will be of value to every citizen of this State. We are *now* willing to confess, that when we fired the first gun in this legal warfare, we did it with some misgiving and doubt as to how far the canons of the law would support us. Yet from the first, we were sustained with the consciousness that in our position we *were right*, and that justice and equity threw at least a kindly cloak around us. It has been this principle of justice and right that has finally triumphed over the obsolete technicalities of the law which originated in the dark ages, at a time when the king owned the subject, and individual rights were considered to be of but little consequence.

Our opponents will doubtless say that it illustrates simply the uncertainties of the law. Surely in this they are much mistaken. If ever in the history of the jurisprudence of this State, there has been a case which clearly established the *certainty* and inflexible justice of the law, it is seen in the case just decided.

We knew that in good faith we had entered into an important contract with Dr. Chase, and had staked a handsome fortune upon that contract. We knew that, at the time, Dr. Chase made that contract in good faith. Ere long, we saw him and five others in open violation of that contract, attempting to rob us of that which he had sold to us, and for which he had our money. We saw him doing that which ought to have placed him and his coadjutors in the confines of a penitentiary. We saw them doing that which, if we had not had ample means and some small degree of "pluck," would have caused our utter ruin. We marveled at their dishonesty and fraud, and asked, Is there no redress? And from the lips of the masses there came the one answer, "*No*. The contract you made with Dr. Chase is worthless. He and his conspirators have consulted the brightest legal minds in the country, and they all say: Mr. Beal, you have no remedy. The law of many centuries is against you. It ought not to be so, but it is so."

"Notwithstanding all these adverse winds," we were not entirely discouraged. The thought would come upon us, that possibly some of these wise and infallible men of the law might be mistaken in their construction of it, and that we ought to make the fight. And we commenced with a will and a determination to see whether the law under which we live was only a bundle of absurdity and inconsistencies. The result shows that those wise men of law were simply wise in their own conceit. Their exposition of the law was only a warping and torture of its principles.

When the first victory came, what groans and lamentations! What charges and accusations! What invective and billingsgate were launched against the innocent and conscientious head of Judge Crane! How freely, how openly, how *dastardly*, our opponents charged Judge Crane with bribery and corruption!

Let the tongues of these *miserable* men, whose mouths were filled with the "purchase and sale of Judges," now be silent. They to-day stand, in the eyes of the people of this county and district, rebuked for their calumny and villifications. The Supreme Court, composed of as pure men as ever sat on the woolsack, affirm and endorse Judge Crane in *every respect*, so far as the *merits* of this cause are concerned.

Will the distinguished (alas! *extinguished*) astronomer, and his confreres in this fight, enter our public streets and now openly charge that we have bought and corrupted the Supreme Court? What now will be their war cry?

We candidly believe that we speak the sentiments of an unanimous and outraged public, when we assert, that so far as honesty of purpose, of purity of intention, of rigid adherence to right, truth and justice in the discharge of his judicial duties, are concerned, the name of Judge Crane will be fresh and green in the memory of the people of this county, when his revilers and calumniators will be remembered only with scorn and ridicule.

It has been a long and expensive litigation. Those who have battled for us in this contest, have done their duty well. We have settled for you, my friends, one and all, an important principle of the law, which will be of daily value to you. The law of this country will be no longer mooted on the subject of contracts in restraint of trade. The happy days of those who have been pleased to make and break these contracts at their pleasure, are ended. To my opponents and their counsel, whose smiles of derision have so often lighted the darkness of their reverses, and whose ripples of laughter are now changed to unavailing wailings, and to whose rescue we cannot now come, we make to you our adieus, until we meet again to settle some other matters, with this recommendation: that you study carefully the old and honored maxim, "*Honesty is the best Policy.*"

Printed in Dunstable, United Kingdom